D1441022

S H A K E R

The Art of Craftsmanship

S H A K E R

The Art of Craftsmanship

The Mount Lebanon Collection

Timothy D. Rieman
with an essay by Susan L. Buck

Art Services International
Alexandria, Virginia

1995

TABLE OF CONTENTS

PARTICIPATING MUSEUMS

The Chrysler Museum
Norfolk, Virginia

High Museum of Art
Atlanta, Georgia

Wadsworth Atheneum
Hartford, Connecticut

Sheldon Memorial Art Gallery
and Sculpture Garden
University of Nebraska
Lincoln, Nebraska

Columbus Museum of Art
Columbus, Ohio

Delaware Art Museum
Wilmington, Delaware

Wichita Art Museum
Wichita, Kansas

This exhibition is organized and
circulated by Art Services International,
Alexandria, Virginia

Copyright © 1995 by Art Services International
All rights reserved

All objects are part of the Mount Lebanon
Shaker Collection. In the object entries of
the catalogue, height precedes width
precedes depth.

LIBRARY OF CONGRESS
CATALOGING-IN-PUBLICATION DATA

Rieman, Timothy D.
    Shaker : the art of craftsmanship : the Mount Lebanon collection /
Timothy D. Rieman with an essay by Susan L. Buck.
        p.   cm.
    Catalog of an exhibition organized and circulated by

 Art Services International, Alexandria, Va; participating museums,
the Chrysler Museum, Norfolk, Va. and others.
    Includes bibliographical references.
    ISBN 0–88397–109–7
    1. Decorative arts, Shaker—Exhibitions. 2. Decorative arts—New
York (State)—New Lebanon—Exhibitions. 3. Mount Lebanon Shaker
Village (New Lebanon, N.Y.)—Exhibitions.   I. Buck, Susan L. (Susan
Louise), 1954–   . II. Art Services International. III. Chrysler
Museum.   IV. Title.
    NK838.N34R54   1995
    745'.08'8288—dc20
                                                                94-36405
                                                                CIP

PHOTOGRAPHER: Mark Daniels
EDITOR: Nancy Eickel
DESIGNER: The Watermark Design Office
PRINTER: Craft Print Ltd.

ISBN 0–88397–109–7

Printed and bound in Singapore

COVER: Details of counter
(cat. no. 12) and
basket (cat. no. 49)

FRONT AND BACK ENDSHEETS:
Details of alphabet board
(cat. no. 45)

FRONTISPIECE: Detail of cupboard
over drawers (cat. no. 6)

PAGE 6: Detail of pitchfork
(cat. no. 69)

PHOTOGRAPHY CREDITS:
Courtesy of Hancock Shaker Village, Hancock, Massachusetts:
    photograph on page 32
Courtesy Historic American Buildings Survey, New York State:
    line drawings on pages 20, 22, 23
Courtesy New York State Library, Albany: photographs on pages 16, 27
Courtesy Timothy D. Rieman: line drawings on pages 14, 32, 37–43
Courtesy Paul Rocheleau: photographs on pages 176–177, nos. 1–12
Courtesy Shaker Museum and Library, Old Chatham, New York:
    photographs on pages 18–26, 28, 70, 73, 90, 101, 103, 113, 115,
    119, 121, 151, 153, 161, 164, 173

Board of Trustees of Art Services International

James M. Brown III

Roma S. Crocker

Stephen S. Lash

Jean C. Lindsey

DeCourcy E. McIntosh

Mrs. Richard Mellon

Mark Ormond

Robert D. Papkin

Richard B. Pfeil

Mrs. John A. Pope

Lynn K. Rogerson

David Saltonstall

Joseph W. Saunders

Francesca von Habsburg

ACKNOWLEDGMENTS

An aura of mystery has long surrounded the United Society of Believers, popularly known today as the Shakers. From the founding of this religious sect in eighteenth-century England to the closing of several Shaker communities in the late 1940s, the Shakers forged a peaceful and self-sustaining existence. Believers initially shunned contact with "the World," which fueled speculation as to their "plain and simple" practices. By the mid-nineteenth century they had developed complicated systems for producing furniture, clothing, fruits and vegetables, and medicinal items for themselves, much of which they also marketed to outsiders. With the decline of the Shakers, popular culture has often misconstrued their beliefs, practices, and accomplishments even further. A close examination of the exceptional craftsmanship of the furniture they made for themselves at Mount Lebanon, New York—a principal Shaker community and the seat of the Shakers' religious authority—illuminates the level of their artistic achievement and the variety of their efforts. It is with pleasure that Art Services International introduces the creativity of the Mount Lebanon Shakers to audiences throughout the United States. In doing so, we hope that the sophisticated art of these craftsmen and their artistic legacy will be more widely recognized.

One of the leading figures today in the preservation of Shaker history is Ken Hakuta. With great foresight he has saved and is conserving for posterity much of the physical record of the Mount Lebanon Shakers. His keen interest in the Shakers and his personal dedication to promoting their craftsmanship deserves our highest praise, and we thank him and his wife, Marilou Hakuta, for the opportunity to share the Mount Lebanon Shaker Collection with others. We send Mr. Hakuta our personal thanks for his infectious enthusiasm and his generosity.

Timothy D. Rieman has added an exciting chapter to our understanding of the Shakers by critically examining their furnituremaking techniques and the way that Shaker production of chairs and cupboards meshed with their religious beliefs and communal practices. As Guest Curator of the exhibition and a recognized authority on Shaker furniture, Mr. Rieman selected the objects and has offered great insight into their manufacture. We congratulate him on the successes of his research and send to him our warmest regards. It has truly been a pleasure to work with him.

We are pleased to acknowledge the pioneering work of furniture conservator Susan L. Buck, who conducted scientific analysis on several pieces in the Mount Lebanon Shaker Collection. Such microscopic examination of Shaker finishes has rarely been undertaken. We are pleased to introduce her findings in this catalogue, which will be of interest to Shaker scholars and collectors alike, and we thank her for her contributions.

It is gratifying that our enthusiasm for the art of Shaker craftsmanship is shared by so many others in the museum community. With great pleasure we recognize the following key individuals at the art institutions which have joined in the exhibition's tour: Robert H. Frankel, Director, and Mark Clark, Curator of Decorative Art, at the Chrysler Museum in Norfolk, Virginia; Ned Rifkin, Director, and Donald Pierce, Curator of Decorative Arts, at the High Museum of Art, in Atlanta, Georgia; Patrick McCaughey, Director, and Kristin Mortimer, Deputy Director, at the Wadsworth Atheneum in Hartford, Connecticut; George Neubert, Director, and Daphne Deeds, Curator and Assistant Director, at the Sheldon Memorial Art Gallery and Sculpture Garden at the University of Nebraska-Lincoln; Irvin Lippman, Executive Director, and Nannette V. Maciejunes, Senior Curator, at the Columbus Museum of Art in Columbus, Ohio; and Stephen T. Bruni, Executive Director, and Jenine Culligan, Associate Curator for Exhibitions, at the Delaware Art Museum in Wilmington, Delaware; and Inez Wolins, Director, and Novelene Ross, Chief Curator, at the Wichita Art Museum in Wichita, Kansas.

Successfully melding written word and visual image were Nancy Eickel, Don and Lynne Komai, and Mark Daniels. As editor, designers, and photographer, they pooled their talents to produce a book that reflects the sophistication of the Shakers' world. Working with the printing firm of Craft Print Ltd., their efforts have resulted in a handsome volume, and we congratulate them on a task so skillfully accomplished.

Once again it is our honor to recognize the dedication and professionalism of the staff of Art Services International—Ana Maria Lim, Douglas Shawn, Anne Breckenridge, Kirsten Simmons, Betty Kahler, Patti Bruch, and Sally Thomas—whose collective and individual efforts have brought this project to realization. Their focused attention to all aspects of this exhibition and their continued good humor merit our highest praise.

Lynn K. Rogerson
Director

Joseph W. Saunders
Chief Executive Officer

INTRODUCTION

Since the eighteenth century, the Shakers have prevailed as one of the best known and longest lived of all religious communal groups in the United States. Many of the beliefs, traditions, and practices to which the Shakers adhered were initiated by a small group of Shaking Quakers who arrived in the American colonies from Manchester, England, in 1774. Led by their spiritual mentor Mother Ann Lee, the Shakers secured a following in New York state and throughout New England. Within the next few decades nineteen long-term communities were in existence in eight states as far west as Kentucky.

The first Shaker community was founded at New Lebanon, New York, with the construction of a meetinghouse for worship in 1785. Other buildings essential for communal living were erected there over the next decades. The model community of New Lebanon quickly rose in prominence as the spiritual center of the Shakers and the home of their central ministry. (The location was renamed Mount Lebanon in 1861; the Shakers referred to it as simply "The Mount.")

At Mount Lebanon, as in other Shaker villages, Brothers and Sisters practiced the daily routines and religious precepts that defined their new lives as members of the United Society of Believers, the formal name that the Shakers adopted in 1826 to underscore the unity of their doctrines, laws, and rituals. Converts staunchly believed in physical separation from "the World," celibacy, and common property. An essence of simplicity and a singleness of heart allowed them to focus their individual and collective energies on leading spiritual lives. In creating their version of heaven on earth, the Shakers promoted the virtues of faith, hope, honesty, innocence, meekness, humility, pacifism, patience, thankfulness, and charity.

They also encouraged industry and disdained those who were idle. The Shakers at Mount Lebanon developed numerous trades, from raising herbs to sustain a large pharmaceutical market to operating a nationally known chair manufactory and producing scores of sewn items that were offered to an extensive tourist trade. For themselves, they constructed buildings for protection, made clothing for their bodies, grew food for their physical nourishment, manufactured medicines for their ailments, and built furniture to equip their work and living spaces.

Physical labor was also an integral part of their spirit-filled lives. They literally built by hand their own small world, constructing and developing their communities to suit their needs. Meetinghouses, with separate entrances for men and women, were erected first to fill their spiritual requirements. Dormitory-like structures, administrative offices, barns, laundry houses, and other facilities were built as the community demanded. Each room within the vast complex at Mount Lebanon had to be furnished, and the craftsmen and women met the challenge with exceptional results.

Spirituality as defined by the Church ministry directed all aspects of the Shakers' lives, including the design and construction of furniture. Before 1800, the basic concepts of plain and simple living and of work well done were endorsed by the leadership at Mount Lebanon. Even at this early stage, the Shakers dismissed ostentatious displays of decoration and superfluous ornamentation as being detrimental to the single pursuit of a spiritually fulfilling life.

Variations in Shaker furniture styles often reflect regional differences and changes within the spiritual community. The "classical" period of the 1820s led to the revivalism of the 1840s, which dictated styles well into the

"New York State. The Shakers of New Lebanon - Religious Exercises in the Meetinghouse." Published in *Frank Leslie's Illustrated Newspaper* on November 1, 1873.

1860s. By the 1870s, however, elements of Victorian design were evident in the intermixing of woods, bold colors, and fancy moldings. In 1875, a great fire at Mount Lebanon destroyed eight Family buildings and the belongings of scores of Believers. Not only did this create an immediate demand for a huge quantity of furnishings, but it also eliminated much of the furniture produced by Shakers in earlier decades. With the acceptance of commercially manufactured chairs, little furniture was made at Mount Lebanon after 1880.

At its peak in the mid-nineteenth century, the population of Mount Lebanon grew to six hundred members and consisted of eight Families spread along the Taconic Valley and across the New York state line into Hancock, Massachusetts. By the 1860s, however, the Shakers found it increasingly difficult to isolate themselves from the outside world. Changing times forced them to evolve, yet the Shaker membership continued to decline in number. The aging of the Believers, compounded by financial tribulations that intensified throughout the Great Depression, eventually led to the closing of the Shaker community at Mount Lebanon in 1947.

Mount Lebanon
Shaker Village,
late nineteenth century

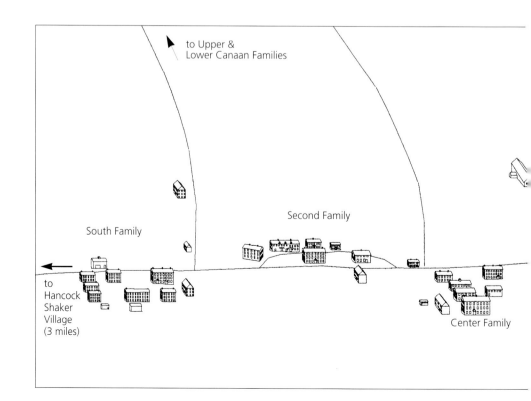

Shakers are probably best known today for the objects they made. Yet it is the humble objects made for personal use that most clearly reflect the Shaker concept of "plain and simple" living. Craftsmen filled the community's needs by constructing benches for meetinghouses, long counters for tailoring, tall cupboards and cases of drawers for storage, and desks for classrooms. Recent scientific analysis of the paints and varnishes used now reveal innovations in technique that have been little appreciated. The simplicity of Shaker design may belie the sophistication of the construction methods practiced by Brothers Isaac N. Youngs, Amos Jewett, Orren Haskins, Amos Stewart, Giles Avery, David Rowley, and many others at Mount Lebanon. This presentation of furniture and objects from the Mount Lebanon Shaker Collection serves as a tribute to the Shakers, who, in their abandonment of beauty, elevated craftsmanship to an art form.

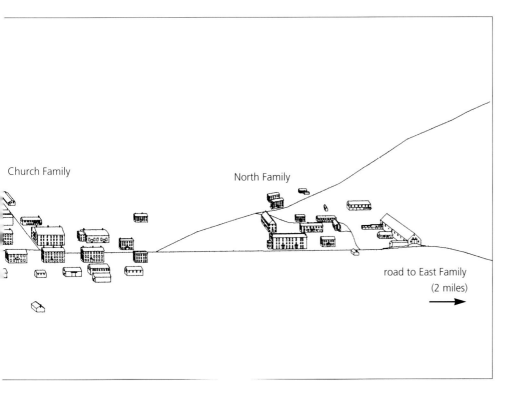

Church Family

North Family

road to East Family
(2 miles)

THE PHOTOGRAPHER'S VIEW

Mount Lebanon Shaker Village

Unidentified photographer, ca. 1870
The second meetinghouse at Mount Lebanon, erected around 1824, was built to replace the original gambrel-roofed meeting-house that dated to 1785. The Shaker ministry resided in the smaller, front section of the building. The unusual barrel roof was constructed with trusses so interior supports would not interfere with the Shakers' dances.

As outside observers of the Shaker community, it is much easier for us to learn of their fine furniture, pharmaceutical industry, and architecture than it is to know the true essence of their beliefs. Chairs and cupboards tell but a small part of the Shakers' story. They represent merely one aspect of the Believers' lives, spent in a community removed from the world.

Historic photographs can help recreate the setting of the Shaker village at Mount Lebanon, New York, of 1870 or 1880. The Church Family had grown under the able leadership of Joseph Meacham, Lucy Wright, Rufus Bishop, Ruth Landon, and Giles Avery. By 1870, the North Family had several outspoken members in leadership roles, including Brother Frederick Evans and Sister Anna White. Mount Lebanon was an active community of over 300 Believers, yet this was actually a decrease in population from the 500 to 600 members it had claimed in the 1860s.

The Shaker communities at Canterbury and Sabbathday Lake included Believers who photographed hundreds of candid images of daily life there. Most images of Mount Lebanon are by worldly photographers. Consequently, images of Mount Lebanon are somewhat more formal views of the village, although interior scenes show the Brothers and Sisters in their work and living spaces. Studio portraits of individuals and groups often convey the strength and compassion of the Shakers.

Photograph by James Irving, New York, ca. 1880

Taken from the North Family barn looking south, the dwelling of the North Family is the largest building on the left, behind the Sisters' shop. The granary, wash house, and infirmary are in the middle ground, with a barn, the hirelings' residence, and the Brothers' workshop on the right. Buildings of the Church Family are in the background.

Unidentified photographer, September 1881
This view of the Second Family's buildings
was "taken on [the] bridge between the corn
house and dry kiln looking north into the
back street. Sept 1881 2nd front left chair
shop, 2nd from rt. Dwelling, extreme Right,
sisters shop of stone."

Photograph by John Williams, ca. 1940
The North Family barn, constructed around
1859, as seen from the northwest.

Photograph by James Irving, New York, ca. 1870
The Church Family dwelling, the large building on the left, was destroyed in the disastrous fire of February 1875, which burned seven other buildings to the ground. Behind the dwelling are the meetinghouse and a workshop. On the right are a dwelling, the infirmary, and the Trustees' office.

Numerous visitors were attracted to Mount Lebanon throughout its history. Many shared their experiences with their families and friends; others wrote articles for periodicals. Blasphemous views abounded. Some writers presented their feelings and opinions in an even-handed manner; some were needlessly positive. Books were also written that focused on the Shakers. *The Communistic Societies of The United States* (1875) by Charles Nordhoff provided a rather informative and scholarly perspective. Yet the nineteenth-century photographer came the closest to fashioning a truthful image of the Shakers.

The most commonly seen photographs of Shaker communities are those taken by William Winters, a professional photographer from Schenectady, New York, who recorded images in the 1930s under the direction of Edward Deming and Faith Andrews. His vivid photographs, however, were often contrived scenes that reflected Edward and Faith Andrews' preconceived notion of Shaker life. Rather than document actual room settings and furniture in situ, Winters carefully arranged objects into still life scenes that perpetuated the idea of the Shakers' "plain and simple" furniture.

Years earlier in the 1870s, photographers J.E. West, James Irving, and others created images that more closely adhered to existing reality. They labored behind their large view cameras, recording scenes of the Shakers in their homes and work places at Mount Lebanon. Certainly they too were selective in their choice of which person, object, or view to document, but a certain objective truth emanates from their photographs. With their practiced eyes, they saw what others overlooked and recorded scenes that no longer exist today. Many of the Shaker buildings are gone, as are all the Believers who appeared before the camera lens. By preserving bits of truth, these photographs have helped the Believers live longer than the pious people and bustling community of Mount Lebanon itself.

Unidentified photographer, ca. 1870
Standing behind a second dwelling or an
infirmary is the large North Family residence.
The photograph was taken from the brick
Brethren's shop. Drawings show the North
Family residence (left) and the meetinghouse
(opposite page) as they appeared in 1961.

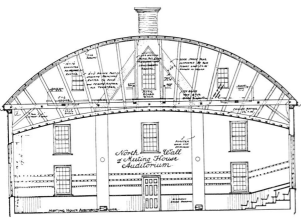

Photograph by James Irving, Troy, New York, ca. 1880
Penciled on the back of this photograph are the words "Looking Northwest across the street from the Infirmary by the corner of the 1st orders Dwelling house. Seed shop (1st Meetinghouse) beyond." The Sabbath often brought many curious onlookers from "the World" to watch the Shakers' unique worship services.

Sarah Beyer and Catherine Allen
(ca. 1850–1922)
An outspoken member of the North Family, Sister Catherine staunchly advocated social and political reforms, including universal suffrage, compulsory education, free legal assistance, and animal rights. She served in the Shakers' central ministry from 1908 until her death.

Unidentified photographer, 1888 (detail)
Believers posed on the south entrance of the meetinghouse, Mount Lebanon, New York

Photograph by the Richardson studio, Brooklyn New York, ca. 1880
As leaders in the North Family, Eldresses Antoinette Doolittle (1810–1886) and Anna White (1831?–1910) espoused the issues of women's rights and world peace. Many progressive Shakers endorsed equality between the sexes, both within Shaker communities and beyond.

Photograph by N.E. Baldwin, 1940 (right) Sister Lillian Barlow (1856–1942) was among the last of the Shakers who continued to manufacture chairs. She is pictured here in the Second Family's chair shop, where she had worked for more than two decades.

As natural and Shaker sisters, Emma Neale (1847–1943) and Sadie Neale (1849–1948) were often photographed together. Posed behind them is "Sister Carrie."

Photographed by Sterry & Co., Albany, New York, ca. 1870?
A devoted socialist, Brother Frederick Evans (1808–1893) was one of the most outspoken and well known of the late nineteenth-century Shakers. He wrote and lectured widely on land rights, the right to vote, the separation of church and state, and world peace.

Anna White (1831?–1910), in conjunction with Leila S. Taylor, wrote *Shakerism, Its Meaning and Message* (1904), which detailed the history and religious beliefs of the Shakers as they entered the twentieth century.

Giles Avery (1815–1890) not only made furniture at Mount Lebanon, but he also served in the central ministry of the United Society of Believers for more than thirty years. Assuming a leadership position in 1860, Brother Giles represented a new generation of Shakers who struggled with declining memberships and the escalating costs of operating their communities.

A general view of the Mount Lebanon Shaker community as seen from the southwest. The South Family chair shop, which dates from 1872, is partially visible on the left. From the right are the buildings associated with the Second, Center, and Church Families, and in the background are those of the North Family.

SHAKER DESIGN

Superfluities Doomed

Timothy D. Rieman

Until recently, many people who became intrigued by Shaker design were wooed by the superb examples of Shaker furniture encountered in Shaker village museums, as well as galleries and private collections. The result has been a kind of seduction. Charmed and even intrigued by individual pieces, many admirers came to accept select forms and particular objects as being typical of Shaker design. Yet these remarkable pieces can hardly be taken as representative of the Shaker aesthetic.

This narrowed view produces a superficial understanding of Shaker design. Only by moving beyond well-known objects can a broader appreciation be attained. Important sources for research include journals, account books, and the rules and regulations by which the Shakers lived. Their publications, along with the accounts of visitors to their communities and certain recent secondary publications, are often illuminating as well.

One key standard for evaluation—the investigation of actual, everyday objects—is harder to apply. Much evidence of Shaker life and work has been lost to renovation and fire, and the perspective of communal activity has been diluted by the wide dispersal of Shaker goods. Despite the impressive number of artifacts that still exist, the survival rate of Shaker furniture and other objects of their design is quite low. In fact, the very best of Shaker furniture may have been destroyed in the disastrous 1875 fire that consumed eight Mount Lebanon Church Family buildings, along with all the furniture and belongings of the Shakers who lived and worked in them.

This conjecture raises difficult questions. How do the existing objects compare with those that have been destroyed or dispersed? And if they were available for viewing, how would these missing works affect our perception of Shaker design? While these questions cannot be readily answered, the issues they raise may point us in a useful direction in looking at Shaker design.

Certainly any selection of extant objects will influence our understanding and appreciation of Shaker design. The curator, scholar, or writer will likely select the best, most colorful, most unusual, or most appealing works available. Evaluation is thus biased by the selector's personal tastes and by the prevailing aesthetic of the time. It is admittedly impossible to extract ourselves from our late twentieth-century sensibilities. The original artistic intentions of these largely anonymous craftsmen are usually unknown. Thus, our perception of a table or chair, unlike that of its creator, forms the starting point for evaluation.

Such subjective measure is further skewed by the fact that we are of "The World," observers from without rather than Believers within the Shaker community. Consequently, we see objects out of their initial contexts, approaching them from an angle quite different from that of the original user for whom the object was made. In one sense, our detached perspective can be an advantage. An object's intrinsic form can often be more easily discerned when perceptions are not colored by knowledge of the piece's original purpose or function. Appreciation of its beauty may also be less clouded. The Shakers did not primarily concern themselves with beauty per se. Instead, they valued function, regarding a desk, cupboard, door handle, or dipper primarily as a useful object. Function generally took precedence in the mind of the craftsman over the aesthetic qualities of a piece.

Conversely, our secular, twentieth-century approach leads us to perceive most Shaker objects first on their aesthetic appeal, with function often ranking second. A stack of oval boxes placed on a table in a collector's living room may serve as a decorative object. For the owner, the tower of boxes, with its interplay of size, form, and color, may be viewed as sculpture. In contrast, the Believers would have viewed them as a product to be used or sold, or occasionally as a gift to be presented to another Brother or Sister.

Believers saw a work counter as a functional piece of furniture in which to store materials or tools or to provide a broad work surface. That same counter, in the hands of a collector, is more often displayed as an artwork valued for its craftsmanship and intrinsic beauty. Since visual and decorative concerns may be paramount to a collector, the work counter causes a highly different interchange with its modern surroundings than it would have in a nineteenth-century workroom. When viewed as sculpture, the counter may retain its own internal harmony or visual balance, but the original interplay between craftsman and user is inexorably altered.

What was the aesthetic intent of the Shakers? Was it their intention to create beauty or art? In the 1860s, Elder Frederick Evans replied to a question posed by journalist Charles Nordoff, a visitor to the Shaker community, as to "whether if they would build anew, they might not aim at some architectural effect, some beauty of design." Brother Frederick responded unequivocally, "No, the beautiful, as you call it, is absurd and abnormal. It has no business with us. The divine man has no right to waste money upon what you would call beauty, in his house or his daily life, while there are people living in misery."[1] While Brother Frederick, an espoused socialist and Shaker, was likely reacting to the excesses of the Victorian era, his answer probably would not have been much different if the question had been asked of an Elder or Eldress in the 1820s, during the so-called classical era of Shaker design. Beauty was not the primary goal of the craftsmen's endeavors. Indeed, superfluous ornament was viewed as an impediment to the spiritual life.

The joiner and furnituremakers who became Believers in the early days were primarily first- or second-generation immigrants of English origin. They inhabited the northeastern section of the country, in present-day

Figure 1.
This tall case of drawers, dated 1809, was probably built at Mount Lebanon.

Massachusetts, Connecticut, eastern New York, Vermont, New Hampshire, and Maine. Into the Shaker communities they brought their inherent conventions, traditions, behavior, and aspirations. Change was slow to occur as they moved from the culture of the colonial era and the Revolutionary War into the new Federal period.

During these times styles of furniture developed, evolving from the ornate curves and shapes of Queen Anne and Chippendale of the late 1700s to the rectilinear forms, neoclassical design elements, and intricate inlay work of Hepplewhite and Sheraton that were introduced from England around 1800. The major centers of London, Boston, New York, and Philadelphia certainly influenced the growth and dispersion of furniture designs. More immediate influences upon Shaker design, however, were the vernacular designs and forms that distinguished the areas surrounding the Shaker communities or marked the particular regions from which the Believers came. Local or regional furniture designs utilized straightforward, basic concepts with a minimum of extraneous detail, such as tables with tapered legs, cupboards with one or two doors, chests with bracket bases, and simple six-board blanket boxes. For the most part, surfaces were simply finished with paint or varnishes. Craftsmen who joined the Shakers not only introduced these basic forms and simple styles but also brought with them technical skills and intimate knowledge of furniture construction, which they had learned from their fathers or through traditional apprenticeships.

Among the earliest products of Shaker design that still stand are two buildings constructed before the turn of the eighteenth century—the gambrel-roof meetinghouses at the Sabbathday Lake and Canterbury communities. The built-in furniture made for these meetinghouses offer an instructive record of early Shaker design detail and construction. Pine, a readily abundant local wood, provided the material for the meetinghouses and their basic interior trim work, including cupboards with raised panel doors. Wrought iron H-style hinges were applied to the face of the doors and cases, and opaque dark blue paint was used in a typical eighteenth-century manner. Such details are virtually identical to work done by furnituremakers then living in the countryside around Shaker communities. The Shakers' more innovative and distinctive furniture followed in the years after 1800, when a discernible Shaker "style" emerged.

What did the early Shaker craftsmen who were instrumental in developing Shaker design—notably Benjamin Lyons, Anthony Brewster, Amos Bishop, Samuel Turner, Benjamin Goodrich, Amos Jewett, and David Rowley—know about furniture design and construction? What influenced them to develop the Shaker style that we know today, nearly two hundred years later? What was so different about their religion, environment, and way of living? Some of these questions can be answered with confidence, others with careful speculation.

During her travels through the New England area, Mother Ann Lee offered instruction and spiritual inspiration to her many followers. Before her untimely death in 1784, she provided the spiritual basis for the Shaker community. Her successor as leader of the faith was Joseph Meacham, who, in his *Way Marks,* outlined the Shakers' organizational structure and addressed issues of temporal concern, such as the basic concepts of plain and simple living, which were in place before 1800.

> All work done, or things made in the Church for their own use ought to be faithfully and well done, but plain and without superfluity. All things ought to be made according to their own order and use. . . . We have a right to improve the inventions of man so far as it is useful and necessary, but not to vain glory or anything superfluous. Plainness and simplicity in both word and deed is becoming the Church and the people of God. Order and conveniency and decency in things temporal.[2]

These early written design guidelines, endorsing "plainness and simplicity . . . in things temporal," defined and regulated Shaker design in the years that followed. Since the ministry offered divinely inspired guidance in virtually all decisions, temporal as well as religious issues were interpreted through the ministerial leadership of Mount Lebanon.[3]

Little of the dated furniture from the early 1800s is extant. Two pieces— a tall case of drawers dated 1809 and now in the collection of Hancock Shaker Village (fig. 1), and a cupboard over case of drawers inscribed 1817 and now owned by the Society for the Preservation of New England Antiquities (SPNEA) (fig. 2)—indicate that the development of a plain and simple style was well underway two to three decades after the opening of the first Shaker community at Mount Lebanon. The vertically proportioned case of drawers retains a simple applied bracket base, yet it differs from its common counterparts in that its maker incorporated no cornice molding, a key factor in its overall lack of ornament and its particularly stark appearance. The cupboard over case of drawers, however, displays a thoroughly developed Shaker form, one that is now considered a prototype of Shaker design for the next half century. The 1817 case with its plank sides sits on simple cut feet and has a quarter-round cornice molding. Interestingly, its form is not generally found in vernacular work.

The Shakers' capacity for adapting furniture styles is evident in a table (private collection) that was originally a colonial tea table. With the Shakers, it was transformed for a more utilitarian purpose, probably as a sewing table (fig. 3). The easily removable ornamentation of ogee-shaped drops was taken off of the aprons. The ornamental shaped apron was supplemented by a simple, straight piece fastened below the remaining original narrow apron to make it wider. The legs were left unaltered, although they did not

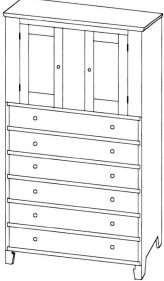

Figure 2.
A drawing of a cupboard over case of drawers, dated 1817, shows the developed "classic" Shaker style.

Figure 3.
Around 1825, the Shakers at Mount Lebanon converted this colonial tea table, circa 1760, into a sewing table.

conform with the Shakers' design repertoire. A drawer was added, along with several small metal balls fastened to the apron, which would have made it possible to hang a sewing bag under the table, as was done in the Federal years. Few objects show so vividly the Shakers' willingness to adapt existing forms to their distinct design parameters.

While many Shaker craftsmen made notations about furniture in their journals, they largely remained silent about the operations of the workshops or the development of their designs. Were they conscious of their designs? Were their aesthetic judgments innate, the products of unschooled but creative minds, or were some craftsmen or members of the ministry, such as David Meacham or Jonathan Walker, formally trained in design concepts and artistic matters? Did the Shakers understand or discuss the ideas of line, balance, and color on a conceptual basis? Or did their conversations center on issues of construction, such as the fit of a drawer or the source of materials?

Some self-consciousness must have been involved. On the drawer bottom of a piece constructed by Brother Henry Hollister in 1861 (The Art Complex, Duxbury, Massachusetts) is the written remark, "Tis only he that has no credit to loose that can afford to work in this style." Evidently Brother Henry had an awareness of design. Clearly, he was not alone.

The *Summary View of the Millennial Church* (1823), written by Calvin Green and Seth Wells, explains the theology of the Shakers. The book summarizes the origins and central precepts of the faith and the way the Shakers focused themselves and their activities in their daily search for spiritually fulfilling lives. It also addresses the importance of the idea of "plain and simple" as it pertains to physical objects in the temporal world. By removing the extraneous, the Shakers hoped to eliminate those things that might confuse or divert attention away from the single pursuit of a spiritual life. They sought

> a real singleness of heart in all our conversation and conduct. . . .
> Its thoughts, words and works are plain and simple. . . . It is without
> ostentation, parade or any vain show, and naturally leads to plainness in
> all things. In all the objects of its pursuit, in all the exercise of its power, in
> all its communications of good to others, it is governed solely by the will of
> God and show forth its peculiar singleness of heart and mind in all things.[4]

The Shakers noted numerous instances of spiritual communication, inspiration, or guidance, though most of those recorded occurred in the 1830s and 1840s, when a mass of written material was accumulated during a revivalistic period. Yet even in earlier decades direct spiritual guidance was received and experiences recorded. One example was offered by cabinetmaker David Rowley.

While plaining at my bench, my whole soul was enshrouded with a mantle of tribulation; but I kept on at my plaining, & soon it appeared to me that my plain began to go with less physical force or exertion on my part than usual. It moved more & more easily until it seemed that I had to hold on to the tool, in order to keep it from moving itself. I thought perhaps it did not take hold of the wood, & so I watched to see if it thru our shavings. I observed it did, but as it still moved without my aid as it were, I questioned the cause, & turned it over to see if it had not caught some little chip or splinter as plains sometimes do, & thus move without cutting; but to my surprise it was all clear. I then concluded it must be driven by some unseen foreign agency or power.[5]

A visitor to the Shaker community in Watervliet, New York, noted, "The Shakers believe that their furniture was originally designed in heaven, and that the patterns have been transmitted to them by angels."[6] Unfortunately, records do not reveal how closely craftsmen related their work to the world of the spirit. Did they often feel the guidance of the spirit as they designed and constructed their furniture?

During the period of revivalism, many instructions that were received through spiritual revelation directly affected Shaker design. One such occurrence in the 1840s was reported in *Shakerism, Its Meaning and Message,* written by Anna White and Leila S. Taylor of the North Family. "At one time, under spirit direction, a general inspection was made of every room and articles of furniture, books, pictures and ornaments were accepted or rejected in accordance with spirit direction."[7] In a journal entry dated 1840, it was reported that Brother David Rowley was "employed for several days in taking out brass knobs and putting in their stead wood knobs or buttons, this is because brass ones are considered superfluous through spiritual communication."[8] Little is known today of this direct spiritual influence, even though it ultimately affected Shaker design and all aspects of Shaker life.

Superfluities doomed to destruction: this simple phrase, found in a Shaker journal dated January 1799, concisely states the direction that Shaker design assumed as the leadership of the Shaker community determined and planned buildings, furniture, clothing, utensils, and other physical aspects of their surroundings. They intended to create objects and indeed an entire physical environment that would help Believers attain spiritual fulfillment.

The Believers had emerged from their initial period of growth by 1800. Their community at New Lebanon had survived for over a decade, much of its rules and organizational structure were in place, and several buildings had been constructed. The major temporal task ahead was the continuous erection of buildings and the provision of furnishings for them. The concept of "plain and simple" continued to be shared in the realm of a spiritual idea, and it was physically expressed in real furniture and buildings.

The Shaker leadership understood how worldly fashions were used. Fancy designs and ornamentation defined status, expressed individual taste, and impressed others. The opulence, formality, and distinct purposes of many furniture forms were rejected by the Shakers, who did not want them to be a part of their lives. The Shakers did not want to just redesign furniture—they were endeavoring to create their own world. They separated themselves from the extraneous influences of the outside world and removed themselves from interaction with non-Believers, from family as they had known it. Men and women related as brothers and sisters, not as husbands and wives. Their new buildings implemented these concepts. The meetinghouse, first constructed at Mount Lebanon in 1785, was followed by residences and workshops. In all of these, much decoration was abandoned in keeping with their desire to separate themselves from the outside world. Extraneous influences on the design of their furniture were regulated and kept secondary to their singleness of purpose as Believers.

Nevertheless, they were aware that buildings, furniture, and material objects have importance beyond their specific utilitarian function. Why else would there be so much color and the use of figured woods in their work? A bird's-eye maple rocker in a retiring room, for example, was far more than a resting spot for an elderly Brother or Sister. A green bed was more than a sleeping platform, a work counter provided more than storage space, and rugs did more than quiet footsteps on a stairway. The shape, size, color, and arrangement of furniture within a room all contributed to a harmonious living environment, and thus affected how Believers perceived themselves and related to others. Perhaps the clearest example of how design directly related to their environment is found in their use of dual entrances and stairways, and their utilization of separate work spaces and dining tables for Brothers and Sisters. Such designs reinforced the physical separation of men and women, and clearly defined their living spaces, much the same way that the lack of ornamentation underscored the concept of "plain and simple."

By 1795 Elder Joseph Meacham had delineated the leadership structure of the Shaker community, which had gathered at Mount Lebanon just ten years earlier. Membership at Mount Lebanon totaled around three hundred persons and was governed by the ministry, which was ultimately responsible for the spiritual well-being of the Believers. In descending hierarchy, the Elders, trustees, and deacons governed the temporal lives of those in each Shaker family, as Believers began to deviate from the norms they had previously known in the outside world. Although the concept of "plain and simple" had originated from the ministry, it was the task of the trustees and the deacons to implement and regulate it.

Many areas of Shaker life, such as clothing, demanded uniformity and careful regulation. Uniformity in the garments of Believers within a community and between communities was deemed extremely important, as is explained in a communication circulated in 1864.

> There are very strong reasons in favor of uniformity, both in style or pattern of dress, and color and quality of dress fabrics: each one, and all of these subjects, effects, materially, the welfare and prosperity of Believers, both spiritually, socially and financially. Spiritually, because uniformity in style, or pattern in dress, contributes to unanimity of feeling; uniformity of color and quality have the same effect, and largely so too; because equality of furnish in dress, between members, contributes to peace and union in spirit, inasmuch as the ends of justice are answered, and righteousness and justice are necessary companions. . . .[9]

Uniformity was sought and enforced throughout Shaker society, even in some of its buildings. Meetinghouses, the first structures built in most eastern Shaker communities, were virtually identical with those built in Mount Lebanon, where the pattern of design and construction was developed, dispersed, and copied exactly. Despite the importance of union and the central role that uniformity played in Shaker life, particular furniture designs varied considerably among communities for many reasons. More variety was allowed in furniture than in clothing and building styles, although simplicity remained of paramount importance.

Shaker design was not, of course, monolithic; it varied considerably from community to community. Some basic forms and small details differed, and each community or bishopric developed its own "pattern" based on the knowledge of its craftsmen and the regional and vernacular styles then in place. Patterns evolved for specific aspects of design, with the basic ladderback chair, for example, being used in most Shaker communities. Individual communities developed distinctive styles in the designs of chair pommels (figs. 4-6), arms, and backslats. Visual patterns also developed for

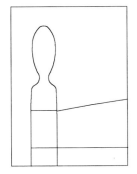 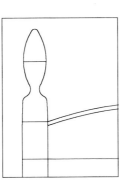 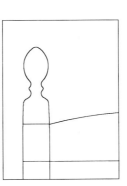

Chair pommels or finials

Figure 4. Canterbury, New Hampshire

Figure 5. Enfield, New Hampshire

Figure 6. Mount Lebanon, New York

case pieces, although the sizes, arrangements, and numbers of drawers or cupboards varied (figs. 7-9). Despite this, construction and finishing details were remarkably similar within a community, which allows many pieces made a century or more ago to be attributed to a particular Shaker community, family, or maker. Those details that were altered more often resulted from stylistic evolution than from a redirection or drastic variation in design.

While furniture forms were generally similar among Shaker communities, regional characteristics made their mark in a variety of details. Furniture produced by Shakers in Kentucky and Ohio, New Hampshire and Maine (figs. 10-13) resemble vernacular styles of their regions. Chairs and cupboards built by Shaker craftsmen in New Hampshire differ from those created by the Brothers in Alfred and Sabbathday Lake, Maine.

It can be said that Shaker craftsmen created a "neo-traditional" or "modern" style by extracting traditional design elements from familiar forms and by excluding superfluous ornament. In doing so, objects were reduced to their basic forms and structure—the case and doors of a cupboard, or the legs, apron, and top of a table. In a sense, the form itself became the ornament. This "modern" look was not easily understood by many worldly observers of the time. They often found the furniture too stark.

Shaker craftsmen felt little need to add decoration to a piece of furniture to deem the work complete. Typical case pieces at Mount Lebanon, for example, consisted of a base—either flat on the floor, or with a cut foot or a simple applied base (figs. 14, 15). The cornice was comprised of a cove, a bullnose, or quarter-round molding. The construction of Shaker furniture

Built-in cupboards with case pieces

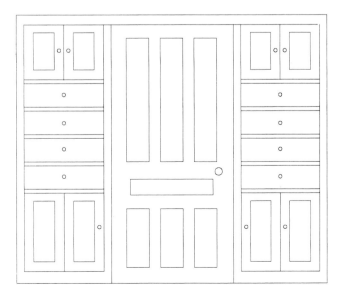

Figure 7. Enfield, New Hampshire

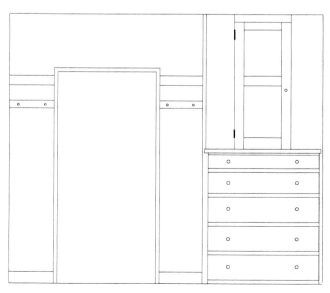

Figure 8. Mount Lebanon, New York

at Mount Lebanon, and its use of mortise-tenon and dovetail joinery, shares much in common with objects built throughout the northeast region of the United States. The sophistication inherent in basic forms stemmed from the needs of a specific community, as well as from the artistic development of the cabinetmakers themselves. While the concept of "plain and simple" was institutionalized through the community rules, it is more likely that apprenticeships and working relationships among joiners provided the innovative and imaginative spark that is peculiar to Shaker design.

What distinguishes Shaker design is its sense of innovation, not its new forms. Furniture was largely created by altering or adapting existing styles. Designs were not driven by client demand but were instead determined by the needs and the relationships among the craftsmen, the deacon or deaconess, and the end user. All was constantly defined by the ministerial precepts that prevailed in the community. Every craftsman well knew that "all things ought to be made according to their own order and use . . . but plain and without superfluity."

Given the extensive and often detailed rules that covered almost every aspect of Shaker life, it is hard to imagine that specific regulations did not address the design of furniture. Such written rules could have been spread by special meetings, daily conversations, and word of mouth through the hierarchy of the Shaker leadership: from the ministry to the trustee and deacon, and from there to the head craftsman of a workshop down to the joiners and young apprentices. The suggestion that implicit rules regarding furniture construction and style did indeed exist is found in a statement made by Brother Thomas Damon to his fellow cabinetmaker Brother

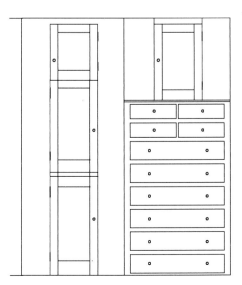

Figure 9. Hancock, Massachusetts

Orders respecting furniture

During the early decades of Shaker furniture construction, many rules were in place, but they were not formalized into written regulations. Below is a speculative set of rules concerning furniture design that might have been in force at Mount Lebanon around 1800. Such verbal rules would have been created by the ministry but were likely enforced within the workshops by the deacons or joiners themselves. Even with these rules, craftsmen were given considerable flexibility in developing forms and applying acceptable ornament.

It is the duty of the Shop Deacons to see that furniture made is in accordance with the orders of the society. Prudence, plainness and economy should prevail.

No new fashions are to be introduced without the consent of the Deacon.

Orders respecting the manufacture of case furniture

1. Case sides and feet should be made with straight lines. Curves are not to be used except in molding.
2. The base is to be built flat on the floor, with a cut foot, or a simple applied bracket foot. There should be no more than one curved element in a bracket foot.
3. Only one or two elements or curves are to be used on any molding.
4. A cornice should extend no more than one inch beyond the case.
5. Drawer fronts are to be made with lips, or rounded and stand proud of the case.
6. Drawer or door pulls shall be simple ones of brass or wood.
7. A case should be built as convenient as possible according to the use of the piece. Doors or drawers can be located at either end according to their use.
8. Color should be of one or more colors of an inexpensive pigment. No flowers or other ornamental painting is to be done.
9. No hidden or excessive joinery is to be used.
10. Fancy woods are not to be used.
11. Turnings on table legs and stands should have no extraneous details.

Figure 10. Case of drawers.
Pleasant Hill, Kentucky.

Figure 11. Storage box with
drawers. Enfield, New Hampshire.

Figure 12. Storage box.
Pleasant Hill, Kentucky.

Figure 13. Tripod stand.
Pleasant Hill, Kentucky.

George Wilcox. In discussing changes in the design of a desk, Brother Thomas stated, "Where there is no law there is no transgression." This implies that some system of design regulations was in place, although it apparently was not an all-inclusive set of rules.

Included within the 1845 Millennial Laws were regulations pertaining to general aspects of Shaker design, furniture, buildings, and such. They were an elaboration or revision of those rules first written in 1821, which dealt superficially with furniture design.

> No new fashions, in manufacture, clothing or wares of any kind, may be introduced into the Church of God, without the sanction of the Ministry, through the medium of the Elders of each family thereof. Fancy articles of any kind, or articles which are superfluously finished, trimmed or ornamental, are not suitable for Believers, and may not be used or purchased; among them are the following; . . . Superfluously finished, or flowery painted clocks, Bureaus, and looking glasses, also superfluously painted or fancy shaped sleighs, or carriages.

> Believers may not in any case or circumstance, manufacture for sale, any article or articles, which . . . would have a tendency to feed the pride and vanity of man. . . .

> Beadings, mouldings and cornices which are merely for fancy may not be made by Believers.

> Odd or fanciful styles of architecture, may not be used among Believers, neither should any deviate widely from the common styles of building among Believers, without the union of the Ministry.

> Varnish, if used in the dwelling houses, may be applied only to the moveables therein, as the following, viz., Tables, stands, bureaus, cases of drawers, writing desks, or boxes, drawer faces, chests, chairs, etc. etc. . . . Oval or nice boxes may be stained reddish or yellow, but not varnished.

Though Shaker forms were virtually stripped of ornament, their designs often became complex and pushed the bounds of traditional concepts of function, balance, and symmetrical design. Innovative asymmetrical design based upon the function of the piece took precedence. This allowed the creation of furniture with doors set opposite drawers (figs. 16, 17) or with drawers of unequal length or depth adjacent to one other (fig. 18). Drawers were rearranged to create a visual balance point rarely seen in worldly furniture. Sometimes drawers were graduated in groups, with three graduated drawers built next to four, rather than each drawer diminishing in depth, as was commonly done by worldly furnituremakers. Lengths of drawers commonly varied within a single piece of furniture.

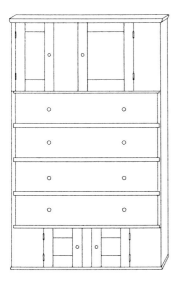

Figure 14.
Cupboard with case of drawers.
Mount Lebanon, New York.

Figure 15.
Storage box with drawers.
Mount Lebanon, New York.

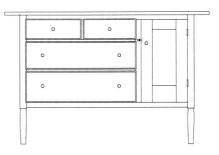

Figure 16.
Sewing counter.
Hancock, Massachusetts.

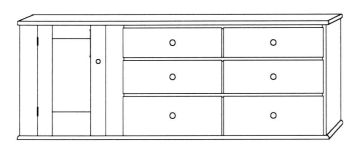

Figure 17.
Counter.
Mount Lebanon, New York.

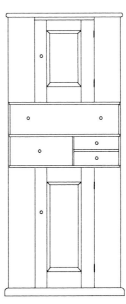

Figure 18.
Cupboard with drawers.
Enfield, Connecticut.

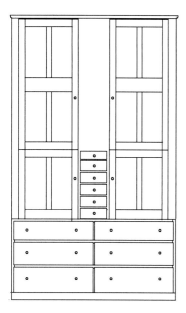

Figure 19.
Cupboard with drawers.
Mount Lebanon, New York.

Gradually new design concepts became new traditions, passed from one workman to another. Some individuals or groups of cabinetmakers within workshops developed styles of consistent restraint or an impeccable use of design concepts, which were continued by apprentices. One craftsman's innovation could become a workshop practice. Through the travels of furnituremakers, such as Elder Grove Wright, who was in the ministry, shop practices became bishopric designs that spread to other communities. Such designs, however, remained idiosyncratic due to the isolation of the Shaker communities, much in the same way as the traditional ethnic work of the Dutch along the Hudson River or the Germans in Pennsylvania was maintained.

Other forms that were occasionally seen in worldly furniture, such as the cupboard over case of drawers, became commonplace in Shaker communities. Innovation led to the elaboration and development of designs that far exceeded the simple one- or two-door cupboards of earlier years. Cupboard doors and drawers were arranged with creativity and sophistication. Although some Shaker designs are awkward or commonplace, many show a masterful interplay of proportion and shape that results in visual balance. One example is a tall cupboard and case of drawers that stood for years at Mount Lebanon (fig. 19). The long vertical panels and six graduated drawers are expertly handled, and the center column of small drawers presumably served a specific function. A large double cupboard over case of drawers, built in Harvard, Massachusetts, shows an intriguing arrangement of drawers. Three shallow drawers over a double column of half-width appear over an identical set of three drawers on the bottom. Also, the doors above are framed in an unusual manner. Such an arrangement might be thought unique, but in the same house is a nearly identical case, except the bottom three drawers are replaced by a single, full-width drawer. The maker of this case must have felt this long drawer was visually out of place, so it was made to look like two half-width drawers. Brother Amos Stewart of Mount Lebanon built several case pieces of roughly the same size that used the same door-over-drawer organization, yet he utilized rather free variations in arranging the drawers (fig. 20).

Judging from extant pieces of furniture, color abounded in the Shaker living and work spaces. Green beds and large yellow and red cupboards and cases of drawers were used. Wall units twelve to fifteen feet in height were finished in bold yellow, as was a fifty-foot long attic at the Shaker community in Canterbury, New Hampshire. Broad areas of bold color were juxtaposed against white plastered walls that were bordered with peg rails running the perimeter of many rooms. Due to the ongoing research into paints and varnishes, the original color of much Shaker furniture, which has often been obscured, can now be better visualized (see Susan Buck's essay "Interpreting Paint and Finish Evidence on the Mount Lebanon Shaker Collection" in this book).

Some of the earliest pieces of Shaker furniture in the east, dating from the 1790s to the 1830s, were coated with opaque finishes that covered the varying woods or grain textures beneath and visually unified the piece. By around 1820 or 1830, however, craftsmen began to change their finishing techniques. Greater amounts of plant resins or shellac were added to the color pigments, which reduced the opacity to more of a wash. While strong colors, such as red ochre, raw sienna, and chrome yellow, were still used, the grain and variations of the wood shown through clearly. This surface treatment with colorful washes gave the furniture a different appearance. The tactile quality of the wood grain below provided additional surface character. Though not used extensively, two colors sometimes enlivened a single piece, such as yellow and red on a butternut case. This juxtaposition of color is found on a series of built-ins made in 1831 in the Church Family dwelling at Hancock, Massachusetts. In other pieces, curly maple was used as a primary wood in counters, wash stands, and chairs. The variations in the maple created a surface quality that was unavailable with opaque finishes.

Colored, transparent finishes were used through the end of the nineteenth century. Due to the decline of the Shaker community, little furniture other than a line of production chairs was made at Mount Lebanon after that time. It is easy to overlook the colorful qualities of Shaker furniture because so much of it has been stripped, refinished, or repainted in the last fifty years. The Shakers, too, refinished their furniture, sometimes because of surface wear or damage, but also because they presumably wanted to change the appearance of a particular piece.

Shaker design, of course, changed throughout the years. One example is the use of paneled doors, which were utilized in early Shaker cupboards but were largely dropped by 1820 in favor of flat panels. The basic forms that were created by 1800 remained popular until the early 1830s, when there might have been some relaxation of the general rules. Traditional forms nevertheless were used for another twenty or thirty years, in part because of the revivalist period of the late 1830s and 1840s. Revivalism brought about a renewed interest in Mother Ann and in spiritual communication with her and with other inspirational leaders of the founding years. This may have led to a desire to return to an earlier, purer time. Consequently, "classical" Shaker designs from the 1820s and 1830s persisted into the 1850s and 1860s. Appropriate ornamentation was apparently re-evaluated as well. Ladderback straight chairs and rockers, tripod stands, small four-leg tables, trestle tables, and cupboards and cases of drawers continued to be made in their original forms, with some refinement occurring in detail work and the creation of lighter pieces. Many changes in design, however, were as much variations in workshop practices as they were distinct evolutions in design.

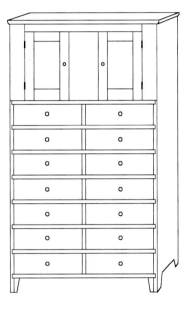

Figure 20.
Cupboard with drawers,
by Amos Stewart.
Mount Lebanon, New York.

The Believers, however, were open to modernization, which is evident in their use of new modes of power for their machinery. They also renovated their dwellings with commercial furniture, including marble sinks with shiny faucets. One Believer may have spoken for many when he stated, "Happily we at Groveland are among the class known as disciples of the new and better way, advocating the best systems of being and doing, thinking and acting."[10] In *Shakerism, Its Meaning and Message,* the Shakers' interest in flexibility and change is clearly stated. "Principles alone are regarded as a fixity; creeds, patterns, forms must in the nature of things be transitory in order to give correct expression to higher conceptions of truth and they constantly adapt modes of thought and action to the progressive principle inherent in the system."[11] As a result, more liberties with furniture design began to be taken. A new era in Shaker design was introduced by crafts-men in several communities: Henry Green of Alfred, New York, Henry Blinn of Canterbury, New Hampshire, and Thomas Fisher of Enfield, Connecticut, as well as by Robert Wagan, manager of the chair industry at Mount Lebanon, along with the older craftsmen at Mount Lebanon, Orren Haskins and Amos Stewart.

The design of chairs produced in the furniture factory at Mount Lebanon was altered in part by the introduction of mass production and the expan-sion of the marketplace to include wholesale customers. Several variations of forms emerged. For years long counters had been utilized in the tailor-ing trades, but now new forms were needed. Galleries were added for storage space on small sewing tables/desks to fulfill new work require-ments. Some sewing desks built after 1870 took on a bold look as the colors of finishes were contrasted on the drawer fronts and the remainders of the cases. Those built ten or twenty years later became more Victorian in character, with their frame and panel designs being well suited to the intermixing of different woods within a single piece. Darker woods such as walnut were used as border moldings around drawers or on case edges to create a conservative yet decidedly Victorian style.

Little furniture was made by Shaker craftsmen at Mount Lebanon after 1880. The great fire at the Church Family in 1875 created an immediate need for quantities of furniture, but for the most part it was contracted to worldly furnituremakers. It is interesting to note that while some design details changed, the precepts of "plain and simple" continued to prevail. Even so, historic photographs of Mount Lebanon from the 1880s show the Shakers using commercially manufactured Victorian furniture, in spite of the existence of numerous pieces of their "old-fashioned" furniture. They simply preferred the new furniture. Brother Oliver Hampton of Union Village may have expressed the feelings of many Brother and Sisters in the late nineteenth century: "Forms, fashions, customs, external rules all have to bow to the fiat of evolution and progress toward that which is more perfect. This need not alarm the most conservative Believer. For unless we keep pace with the progress of the universe our individual progress will be an impossibility. . . ."[12]

Admittedly, for some the elimination of ornament and the concept of "plain and simple" no longer held as much importance as it did in earlier years. Brother Henry Blinn, a noteworthy cabinetmaker at Canterbury, indicated his acceptance of the use of ornament when he described a dwelling he visited in the Shaker community at Pleasant Hill, Kentucky.

> The Brethren's rooms in this dwelling were quite plain and neat. The sisters had taken a little more care for the ornament. A beautifully framed chromo of flowers, and a small framed picture of birds hung from the walls. In one room the table was so filled with fancy articles, trinkets & pictures that we were strongly impressed to regard it as a show case. Really we think this is a good way to make an exhibition of this order of treasures.[13]

The workshop products that are known to have been made by Brother Henry, particularly desks and sewing desks of Victorian design, clearly display the ornament that he apparently enjoyed. For the Shakers, the concept of design had changed forever. Now it is for a new generation of people, those in a modern era marked by a different historic and artistic perspective, to seek again the "plain and simple" in Shaker design.

NOTES

1. Charles Nordhoff, *The Communistic Societies of the Unites States* . . ., 1875, p. 165.
2. "Collection of Writings Concerning Church Order 1791–1796," Western Reserve Historical Society, VIIB:59.
3. The Millennial Laws, which defined the structure and regulations of the Society, were not formally recorded until 1821, even though they probably had been in force for a decade or more under the leadership of Mother Lucy Wright. By then, the general precepts were voiced as the rules became understood and followed by all Believers. Early members who left the community of Believers reported many rules verbatim. According to numerous accounts, regulations were read in general meetings four times each year. These early rules were eventually codified as the Millennial Laws and distributed among communities.
4. Calvin Green and Seth Wells, *Summary View of the Millennial Church*, 1823, p. 347.
5. Jerry Grant and Douglas Allen, *Shaker Furniture Makers*, 1989, p. 17. Western Reserve Historical Society, VB:22.
6. Edward Deming and Faith Andrews, *Religion in Wood*, 1937, p. 17.
7. Anna White and Leila Taylor, *Shakerism, Its Meaning and Message*, 1904, pp. 233–234.
8. "Domestic Journal of Important Occurrences Kept for the Elder Sisters at New Lebanon," Western Reserve Historical Society, VB:60.
9. Giles Avery, "The Circular Concerning the Dress of Believers," 1864, Mount Lebanon, New York. Shaker Museum and Library, Old Chatham, New York, 12025.
10. Stephen J. Stein, *The Shaker Experience in America*, 1992, p. 287. "Home Notes," *Manifesto* 20 (1890), p. 236.
11. White and Taylor, *Shakerism, Its Meaning and Message*, p. 303.
12. Edward Deming and Faith Andrews, *Shaker Furniture*, 1937, p. 51.
13. Andrews, *Shaker Furniture*, p. 53.

Interpreting Paint and Finish Evidence on the Mount Lebanon Shaker Collection

Susan L. Buck

*Things are seldom what they seem
Skim milk masquerades as cream.*

– Gilbert and Sullivan,
 "HMS Pinafore"

In the 1930s, with the encouragement of noted Shaker scholars and dealers Edward and Faith Andrews, interest grew among collectors in the simple, yet elegant furniture of the Shakers and in the objects' original paint colors and finish coatings. The deep reds and intensely colored orange, yellow, salmon, green, and blue paints used on the exteriors and interiors of Shaker furniture provoked curiosity about the unusual Shaker lifestyle and how the choice of a specific color might relate to a particular furniture style or form.[1] Much of what the Andrews believed or guessed about Shaker paints and finishes is now being proven wrong by modern scientific analysis, and today surviving paints and varnishes on Shaker furniture are still frequently misinterpreted or incorrectly identified.

It is not always apparent whether the color on a Shaker piece was intended as a thick, opaque, brushed-on paint layer, or as a more translucent, wiped-on stain. Often this is due to the presence of later varnish layers that obscure the original coatings, or because the colored surface was worn and abraded from regular use, or the object was deliberately stripped and recoated.

In the current literature paint colors are identified by specific pigment names, such as chrome yellow, red ochre, or yellow ochre, when in fact the characteristics of a given paint are based on a number of factors, including the combinations and varieties of pigments, the choice of binding medium, the viscosity of the paint, and the addition of a plant resin or shellac component to enhance gloss. And rarely are shellac clear coatings distinguished from plant resin coatings, which are composed of materials such as mastic, sandarac, damar, copal, and amber.[2]

An 1848–1849 handwritten book of recipes from the Shaker community at Watervliet, New York, inscribed "Rosetta Hendrickson A present from Eld. Austin" and titled *Receipt Book Concerning Paints, Stains, Cements, Dyes, Inks &c.*, contains assorted recipes for interior and exterior paints and varnishes. It also includes notes that indicate where the paints were used, such as "New Lebanon (Chh) Cream Color." Some of the recipes are quite detailed, such as the following recipe for "Fat Copal Varnish."[3]

> Take picked Copal 16 oz.—Prepared Linseed Oil or Oil of Poppies 8 oz.—Essence of Turpentine 16 oz.—Liquefy the copal in a Matrafs over a common fire, & then add the Linseed Oil, or Oil of Poppies, in a state of ebullition. When these matters are incorporated, take the Matrafs from the fire, stir till the greatest heat is subsided; then add the essence of Turpentine, warm.

> Strain the whole while still warm, thro a piece of Linen, and put the varnish in wide-mouth Bottles. Time contributes to its clarification, and the quality grows better.

Right: Detail of cupboard
over drawers (cat. no. 6)

The Spirits of Turpentine should be heated in a tin Kettle, by means of boiling water.

This varnish would have produced a durable, relatively clear, high gloss finish. What is particularly intriguing about this recipe is that it is identical to a recipe for Fat Copal Varnish found in an 1829 edition of *MacKenzie's Five Thousand Receipts*, published in Philadelphia almost twenty years earlier.[4] It is a clear indication that Shakers were using finishing methods of "the World" for their own furniture.

To complicate interpretation of the original appearance of Shaker furniture even further, some objects were stripped and recoated by the Shakers while they were still in use. At other times they were stripped and repainted or varnished after being sold out of the Shaker communities.[5] The Rosetta Hendrickson *Receipt Book* also contains several caustic recipes "To get Paint off from Wood."[6]

Modern Analytical Methods

Recent advances in the fields of paintings and furniture conservation use fluorescence cross-section microscopy techniques. This provides the means to locate and identify original paint and varnish layers, to characterize the binding media of each layer, and to distinguish between early and modern clear finish layers.[7] The information revealed can lead to a greater understanding of the original appearance of early Shaker furniture and help in interpreting the combination of colors used in public and private rooms.

In addition, polarized light microscopy (PLM) was used to identify the pigments in a given paint layer. It was possible to date some painted objects more firmly based on the use of certain pigments, such as zinc yellow, which was not commercially produced until 1850.[8]

Initial research into the coating histories of selected pieces from the Mount Lebanon Shaker Collection provides intriguing clues to the intended appearance of the objects, as well as to the original materials and methods of painting and varnishing. Based on this small group of samples, it is not possible to generalize about which pigments were combined to achieve specific colors. All-encompassing statements cannot be made about the use of certain types of oils, gums, or proteinaceous materials in the binding media, or the presence of early shellac or plant resin varnish coatings.
In fact, this initial study of twelve objects has revealed a remarkable variety of Shaker paint and varnish materials, as well as a range of application methods (see chart 1).

Chart 1
Original Pigments and Binding Media

Object	Pigments*	Binding Media Components
Counter (cat. no. 12)	Red ochre	Oil**
Cupboard (cat. no. 10)	Red ochre, iron oxide red, lampblack, charcoal black	Oil, protein**
Cupboard +	Red ochre, burnt and raw sienna, chrome yellow	Oil
Case of drawers (see appendix, no.7)	Red lead, burnt and raw sienna	Oil
Cupboard over drawers (cat. no. 4)	Red lead, red ochre, chrome yellow, charcoal black	Oil
Case of drawers (cat. no. 9)	Zinc yellow, raw sienna, burnt sienna	Oil**
Counter (cat. no. 13)	Burnt sienna	Oil**
Counter (cat. no. 15)	Chrome yellow, red ochre, red lead, burnt sienna, charcoal black	Oil
Cupboard with drawers and tool brackets (cat. no. 8)	Zinc yellow, iron earth pigments	Proteins, oil
Cupboard over drawers (cat. no. 5)	Barium yellow, red lead, chrome yellow, iron earth pigments	Oil**
Tall clock (cat. no. 1)	None***	Oil
Bed (cat. no. 24)	Chrome green	Proteins, oil, carbohydrates

---

*   Exterior surfaces

**   Preliminary FTIR analysis for the presence of organic components in selected samples was conducted by Richard C. Wolbers at the analytical lab of the Henry Francis DuPont Winterthur Museum.

***   The object appears to have been colored with an organic stain.

\+   Not illustrated

Sample Analysis Techniques

The analysis process began by taking tiny samples of paint and/or varnish from selected pieces of furniture in the Mount Lebanon Shaker Collection. Cross-section samples smaller than a pinhead were taken from representative areas with a scalpel designed for eye surgery. Where possible, the samples were taken from areas adjacent to cracks and losses to limit intrusion into surfaces that remain intact. These samples were cast in polyester resin cubes and examined in cross-section under visible and ultraviolet light at magnifications up to 500X to determine the sequence of layers on top of the wood substrate.[9]

A series of biological stains was also applied to the cross-sections to help characterize components in the binding medium, such as oils, proteins, and carbohydrates. More advanced analytical methods were then used on some samples to identify specific types of inorganic and organic components in the various layers.[10]

The cross-section analysis showed that ten of the twelve objects examined had a sizing, or priming, layer composed largely of plant gum or plant resin varnish as the first layer. One object—the red hanging wall cupboard (cat. no. 10)—was sized with shellac. No sizing layer was present in the cross-sections taken from the green bed.

The sizing material trapped in the wood fibers indicates that the Shakers prepared the wood surfaces by applying a layer of plant gum to seal the wood before applying a paint or stain layer. This means that any subsequent layer would not penetrate deeply into the wood fibers, but would instead form a discrete layer on the surface of the wood. Thus, even if a low-viscosity paint was applied, the pigment particles would tend to be distributed on the surface and would not soak into the wood. This approach not only produces a more intense color, but it is also a frugal way of using expensive pigments. In fact, the cross-sections reveal that the paint layers were often low viscosity and thus formed a thin film on the surface rather than a thick, defined paint layer.[11]

The Green Bed Revealed

The green bed (cat. no. 24) is the only object in this group that has a paint treatment distinctly different from the other objects examined. The wood substrate of the bed was not primed, and two thick layers of green paint, colored solely with chrome green pigment particles, survive.[12] The binding medium in the paint contains oil as well as carbohydrate and protein components, which indicates it may have been an early form of emulsion paint.[13]

Right: Detail of bed (cat. no. 24)

The first deep green paint layer directly on top of the wood is quite opaque. The second, more translucent, green paint layer is well "wet into" the first layer, suggesting that it was applied before the first layer had completely dried. The second layer also contains a plant resin component in the binding medium, as indicated by the recognizable autofluorescence of this layer under ultraviolet light. This would have made the top layer of paint more glossy and durable than the layer below.[14] Such a method of paint application directly relates to correspondence from Brother Daniel Boler at the Ministry at Watervliet to Brother Orren Haskins, cabinetmaker, at Mount Lebanon in 1865: "In the present case as touching the use of Varnish on the wood work of our dwellings in the sanctuary at the Mount, we have unitedly decided to have what varnish is used, put into the last coat of paint. . . ."[15]

Counter Treatments

The counter (cat. no. 13) made by Benjamin Lyon (1780–1870) and/or Charles Weed (1831–left Mount Lebanon 1862) initially appears to have a clear finish, but cross-section analysis and pigment identification of the surviving material show that the original intent was quite different. Trapped in the wood fibers of the counter top, sides, and drawer fronts are remnants of an oil-bound paint or stain (it is not possible, given the limited evidence, to determine how thick this coating was originally) that is colored with burnt sienna pigment particles.

The pigment particles trapped in the wood are covered with three overvarnish layers that were definitely applied in the twentieth century. In fact, the first overvarnish above the wood is a modern synthetic layer, probably a polyurethane varnish. The presence of the burnt sienna particles indicates this counter was originally a rich, deep, glossy red-brown color, very unlike its current clear-finished appearance.[16]

Similarly, cross-section analysis and pigment identification revealed that a frame and panel butternut counter (1860) attributed to Amos Stewart (1802–1884) had been painted or stained with an oil-bound coating composed of chrome yellow, red ochre, red lead, burnt sienna, and a minute amount of charcoal black pigment (cat no.15). Cross-section photographs show that at some point most of the paint or stain layer was removed, then the counter was coated with a modern synthetic resin varnish. The counter was subsequently coated with a layer of shellac and finally with a thick layer of plant resin varnish (see chart 2). This counter was originally an intense, deep orange color, but now it simply appears to have a clear finish.

Detail of counter (cat. no. 12)

Pigment Analysis to Assign Manufacture Dates

Analysis of a large cupboard (ca. 1840; cat. no. 8) that was used for storage of a cabinetmaker's tools revealed a yellow tempera paint layer both on the interior and exterior surfaces.[17] An egg or gum tempera binding medium typically produces a matte, or flat, paint surface. Pigment analysis showed the yellow paint was composed primarily of zinc yellow with a small proportion of iron earth pigments (probably raw and burnt sienna). Zinc yellow, an artificial pigment discovered in 1809 in Paris, was not produced commercially until 1850.[18] If the circa 1840 date for the cupboard is correct, the cupboard was initially left uncoated or was simply sized, and then painted after 1850 when zinc yellow became readily available. Another possibility is that the cupboard was made and painted bright yellow after 1850.

Looking More Carefully at Red Paints

On cursory examination, the red hanging wall cupboard (ca. 1800; cat. no. 10) and the original finish of the red counter (ca. 1820; cat. no. 12) appear to be quite similar in color. The pigment combinations vary significantly, however, and the hanging cupboard was sized with shellac, while the counter was sized with plant gum (see chart 2). The pigments in the paint on the exterior of the hanging cupboard are composed primarily of red ochre, with lampblack, charcoal black, and iron earth red pigments. The paint layer on the counter is composed solely of red ochre pigment particles.[19]

Chart 2
Surviving Clear Coatings

Object	Original Coating	Later Finish**
Counter (cat. no. 12)	Plant resin	*3 layers:* all synthetic resin varnish
Cupboard (cat. no. 10)	*	*2 layers:* 1. synthetic 2. plant resin
Cupboard +	Plant resin	
Case of drawers (see appendix, no. 7)	May have been a plant resin glaze layer on the top and knobs	
Cupboard over drawers (cat. no. 4)	None	None
Case of drawers (cat. no. 9)	Remnants of plant resin	*2 layers:* 1. synthetic 2. plant resin
Counter (cat. no. 13)	*	*3 layers:* 1. synthetic 2. plant resin 3. plant resin
Counter (cat. no. 15)	*	*3 layers:* 1. synthetic 2. shellac 3. plant resin
Cupboard with drawers and tool brackets (cat. no. 8)	*	Remnants of synthetic resin varnish
Cupboard over drawers (cat. no. 5)	Plant resin	None
Tall clock (cat. no. 1)	Plant resin	Plant resin
Bed (cat. no. 24)	Plant resin in the upper paint layer	None

* The object may have originally been unvarnished.
** The designation "1" means it is the first (earliest) overvarnish layer.
+ Not illustrated

Both pieces have been revarnished, which can significantly alter the appearance of a painted surface. The original, thick red paint layer on the counter has been covered with a thin, irregular brown glaze and three layers of synthetic resin varnish. The thin red paint layer on the hanging cupboard has been revarnished with one thin synthetic resin layer above the paint and, most recently, a thin layer of plant resin varnish. As all these coatings age and degrade they become progressively more yellowed and darkened, thus altering the tonalities of the original red paints from bright, intense red to a brown-red color.

Conclusion

This comparative analysis is only the beginning of a more comprehensive study of the paints and finishes used on furniture at Mount Lebanon, but the initial results indicate that the Shakers incorporated a wide range of materials into their coatings. There appear to be no set combinations of pigments or binding media to produce certain colors or effects, and few specific pigments or binders are related to the date of manufacture. Deep red, one of the most commonly occurring colors, could be produced simply by using red ochre in an oil binding medium or by utilizing more complicated combinations of pigments, such as red ochre, iron oxide red, charcoal black, and lampblack, in an oil binder.

Recipes and inventory lists suggest the Shakers used inexpensive and readily available materials, such as linseed oil, obtained from the seeds of the flax plant, and traditional pigments, such as raw sienna, burnt sienna, raw umber, red lead, white lead, iron oxide red, lampblack, yellow ochre, and whiting.[20] They also employed comparatively more expensive materials, such as copal, gum shellac, verdigris (an unstable copper-based green pigment), and Chinese vermilion. The expensive materials may have been reserved for more important furniture and objects, and were applied sparingly on architectural elements.

Current technology allows us not only to identify original coatings more accurately and to distinguish them from later paints and clear coating layers, but also to understand how the appearance of Shaker furniture may have changed over the decades. At the same time analysis reinforces the importance of accuracy in identifying original coatings and underscores the need to develop appropriate descriptions for Shaker paint colors. This type of analysis is particularly important for furniture that has a long history of use because, although the original evidence survives, it is not always visible to the naked eye.[21]

Notes

1. Edward Deming and Faith Andrews, *Shaker Furniture* (New Haven: Yale University Press, 1937; reprint, New York: Dover Publications, Inc., 1964), pp. 116-119.

2. For clarity, the term "varnish" is used to describe all clear coatings. When possible, finish coatings are distinguished by their composition, i.e., shellac, plant resin, or synthetic resin. Recipes for "Fat Copal Varnish" and Mastic varnish are included in Rosetta Hendrickson's *Receipt Book Concerning Paints, Stains, Cements, Dyes, Inks, & c.*, Watervliet, New York, ca. 1848–1849. "Gum shelack" and "shelack" are also included in the recipes and inventory lists in this receipt book.

3. See page 10 of Hendrickson's *Receipt Book Concerning Paints*.

4. See page 23 of *MacKenzie's Five Thousand Receipts in all the Useful and Domestic Arts* (Philadelphia: James Kay, Jun. and Brother, ca. 1829).

5. Charles L. Flint, *Mount Lebanon Shaker Collection* (New Lebanon, New York: Mount Lebanon Shaker Village, 1987), p. 32.

6. See page 15 of Hendrickson's *Receipt Book Concerning Paints* for the following recipe:
   "To get Paint off from Wood"
   Pour about one handful of soda to a quart of water. Let this be applied to the paint, on doors, drawer faces or whatever be required or desired, as hot as possible with a cloth & the better you can apply the Soda & Water, the easier the paint will come off. Care should be taken to not let the wood get wet where there is no paint, lest it become stained. Wash or rinse off with water, and it is done. NB. The soda and water may be used until it is as soap, with paint.

7. Richard C. Wolbers, Nanette T. Sterman, and Chris Stavroudis, *Notes for the Workshop in New Methods in the Cleaning of Paintings* (Santa Monica, California: Getty Conservation Institute, 1990), p. 58.

8. Rutherford L. Gettens and George L. Stout, *Paintings Materials* (New York: Dover Publications, Inc., 1966), p. 178.

9. See Gregory Landrey, "The Conservator as Curator: Combining Scientific Analysis and Traditional Connoisseurship," *American Furniture* (Hanover, New Hampshire: The Chipstone Foundation, 1993), pp. 152–155, and Richard Wolbers and Gregory Landrey, "Use of Direct Reactive Fluorescent Dyes for the Characterization of Binding Media in Cross Sectional Examinations," *AIC Preprints* (Washington, D.C.: American Institute for Conservation of Historic and Artistic Works, 1987), pp. 168–202.

   The samples were examined with an Olympus BHT Series 2 Fluorescence microscope with UV (300 to 400 nm. with 420 nm. barrier filter) and V (390 to 420 nm. with 455 barrier filter) cubes. Each sample was studied under visible and ultraviolet reflected light. In cross-section, under visible light, clear finish layers look uniformly translucent and amber in color, but under ultraviolet light these materials fluoresce with brilliant characteristic colors. For example, shellac glows bright orange, while plant resin coatings (typically combinations of copal, mastic, sandarac, damar, and/or amber) fluoresce bright white or greenish-white. Modern synthetic coatings do not fluoresce like natural resins and generally appear as a dull blue or gray under the ultraviolet light. Accumulations of dirt between layers and the presence of age cracks can indicate that an early coating was exposed and weathered before the next finish layer was applied.

10. The author is working with Amy Snodgrass at the Center for Conservation and Technical Studies, Harvard University Art Museum, and Richard C. Wolbers and Janice Carlson at the Analytical Lab at the Winterthur Museum to conduct further analysis of the inorganic and organic components of the paint and finish layers using Scanning Electron Microscopy (SEM), X-Ray Fluorescence (XRF), and Fourier Transform Infrared Spectroscopy (FTIR) techniques. Funding for this analysis is being provided by the Samuel H. Kress Foundation.

11. This low-viscosity paint might also be called a stain, because it appears to produce a relatively translucent effect that emphasizes the figure of the wood. In many of the samples, however, so little of the pigmented material had survived that it could not be determined whether it was intended as an opaque paint layer or as a more translucent stain.

12. For analysis of the pigments in a paint or stain layer, small scrapings of the paint were removed with a scalpel to identify the pigments. The scraped particles were then permanently mounted on microscope slides with Cargille Meltmount, a nonyellowing resin. When viewed under transmitted, plane polarized light at magnifications up to 1250X, each pigment particle type has characteristic color, shape, size, and optical properties. In this way it is easy to distinguish red ochre particles from red lead particles. See Gettens, *Paintings Materials,* pp. 91–181.

13. U.S. Patent recipes for emulsion paints researched by Richard C. Wolbers include the following recipe from the mid-1800s (pigments are excluded):

Water	200 ml.
Linseed oil	80 ml.
Caustic soda	20 g.
Potato starch	10 g.
Casein	6 ml.

14. Cross-sections from a green bed in the collection of the Winterthur Museum are virtually identical in paint layer structure to the bed in the Mount Lebanon Shaker Collection.

15. Timothy D. Rieman and Jean M. Burks, *The Complete Book of Shaker Furniture* (New York: Harry N. Abrams, 1993), p. 62.

16. See Hendrickson's *Receipt Book Concerning Paints,* page 1. A recipe for a burnt sienna stain in linseed oil first instructs the craftsman to heat raw sienna to produce burnt sienna, and then add approximately four ounces of Chinese vermilion to one pound of the burnt sienna in raw linseed oil. The mode of application is as follows:

   Thin with raw Oil, and apply with a bit of sheepskin, or woolen cloth, (Sheepskin the best:) after which when sufficiently dry — say, 24 hours after staining, rub it off thoroughly.

   This may first be done with the common Corn Broom partly worn, applying it briskly to the stained work, after which, rub off again with a piece of Flannel of woolen cloth.

   It is said that this kind of stain never fades or darkens by age, and when applied to light-colored wood, it gives a kind of Mahogany color; especially when under a coat of varnish.

17. Ralph Mayer, *The Artist's Handbook of Materials and Techniques* (New York: Viking Press, ca. 1981), pp. 214–238. Examples of tempera recipes include the following:

Egg-Oil Emulsion	*Gum Tempera Emulsion*
2 parts whole egg	5 parts gum arabic solution*
4 parts water	1 part stand oil
1 part stand oil	1 part damar varnish (5 lb. cut)
1 part damar varnish	3/4 part glycerin

   * Pour 5 fl. oz. of hot water on 2 ounces of crushed or powdered gum arabic.

18. See Gettens, *Paintings Materials,* p. 178.

19. Pigment identification was conducted by James Martin, Assistant Conservator of Paintings and Research Associate, on December 12, 1991, at the Williamstown Regional Conservation Center in Williamstown, Massachusetts.

20. See Hendrickson's *Receipt Book Concerning Paints,* pp. 1–72.

21. Jerry Grant, former Assistant Director of Collections at the Shaker Museum and Library in Old Chatham, New York, provided enthusiastic support for this project, along with access to a copy of the Rosetta Hendrickson *Receipt Book Concerning Paints* and an opportunity to acquire comparative samples from the furniture collection at the Shaker Museum. Richard C. Wolbers, Associate Professor, University of Delaware, made substantial contributions to the analytical aspects of this project, and the Samuel H. Kress Foundation provided funding for FTIR, XRF, and SEM analysis of selected samples.

1

Tall clock

Cherry, pine, rosewood, brass hinges, painted iron face, organic stain, varnish
Made by Benjamin Youngs, Sr.
(1736–1818)

Painted on dial:
Benjamin Youngs / Water Vliet.
Inscribed in red pencil on the face (probably by Isaac N. Youngs): *1806*
Stamped on the false plate: *Birmingham 1806*
83 x 19 1/4 x 9 1/4 in.

Three Shaker Brothers were noted as leading clockmakers within the New York Bishopric. Two were, in fact, related by blood: Brother Benjamin Youngs, Sr., and his nephew, Brother Isaac Newton Youngs (1793–1865). The third was Brother Amos Jewett (1753–1834). Brother Benjamin belonged to the Shaker community at Watervliet, New York, while Brother Isaac and Brother Amos resided at Mount Lebanon. The numerous extant journals kept by Brother Isaac, who is probably best known as the scribe of the Church Family, provide considerable information about the Mount Lebanon community and his own life as a Shaker. He also wrote a journal about one of his many vocations— clockmaking. He constructed many distinctive wall clocks, including simple wooden wall-hung cases made of butternut, such as those in the collection of Hancock Shaker Village in Pittsfield, Massachusetts. Though related to Brother Benjamin, Brother Isaac claimed in his journals that he learned the trade from Brother Amos Jewett. Only one complete clock, along with a number of other clock parts, are now known to have been made by Brother Amos. According to the count painted on the clock faces, that number could reach at least thirty.

Of the three, Brother Benjamin Youngs, Sr., the maker of this clock, stands out. At least a dozen of his clocks still exist. He learned the trade from his father, Seth

Youngs, Sr. (1712–1761), a clock-maker in Windsor, Connecticut. Several of Seth's clocks, and examples made by Benjamin before and after he became a Shaker, are known. Made in the Connecticut River valley and in upstate New York, these clock cases show in their designs the worldly influences of sophistication and rural simplicity. More importantly for the study of Shaker furniture, they show the evolution of the furniture form from worldly to the rather pure "plain and simple" design associated with the Shakers.

This clock case embodies a knowledge of sophisticated design but does not display it in an extravagant manner. With the exception of the rosewood door facing, the arched bonnet is nearly stripped of decorative features. No reeded columns, brass capitals, or broken arches are found. The waist section of the case shows only a beveled detail and a band of rosewood; the base stands on simple cut feet. The case holds the clock's movement, which was also made by Brother Benjamin. It still strikes on the hour and half-hour, and thus attests to the quality of the fine brass movements produced by seventeenth- and eighteenth-century clockmakers.

2
Cupboard over case of drawers

Pine, poplar, fruitwood knobs,
iron hinges, bone escutcheons,
yellow pigment, varnish
ca. 1850
91 1/2 x 60 x 19 in.

Three distinctive features differentiate this large case piece from many other similar pieces: the design configuration, the case made in two pieces, and the use of the bone escutcheon. Most obvious is the way the craftsman opposed horizontal and vertical masses in the overall design. The horizontal mass in the base is formed primarily by the double tiers of drawers, while the vertical mass above results from the three stiles that flank the two exceptionally long doors. The visual length of the doors is accentuated by the use of only one panel where two might have sufficed. Knobs balance the strong horizontal and vertical elements and unite them into a visual whole.

The construction of the case is unusual. Though many worldly pieces are made in two separate pieces, this practice was not common among the Shakers, even in their large case pieces. Here, the cupboard portion of the case can be lifted free of the drawer case below. Bull-nose molding obscures the joint below. A much smaller but notable detail is the use of bone escutcheons, which is not common in Mount Lebanon furniture. When new, these escutcheons would have contrasted vividly with the original yellow wash on the case. A later varnish has since darkened the case and the escutcheons. The case interior retains its original yellow wash.

3
Cupboard over drawers

Pine, hardwood pulls, iron latches and
hinges, dark stain, varnish
ca. 1830
84 3/4 x 78 x 22 1/2 in.

Beautifully proportioned, this large case piece combines the utility and exquisite design that has come to represent classic Shaker form. The case's vertical mass, with its two long pairs of doors and stiles between them, is visually balanced by the horizontal arrangement of the eight, unusually deep drawers. A simple, half-round molding terminates in a lamb's-tongue end (see below) and divides the two masses. The flat base, rounded drawer fronts, thumbnail edge of the door frames, and the quarter-round cornice molding that finish the piece give it a simple yet elegant appearance, which is characteristic of much of the Shaker furniture made by Mount Lebanon craftsmen.

4
Cupboard over drawers

Pine, iron hinges, fruitwood knobs,
red lead, red ochre, chrome yellow,
and charcoal black pigments, varnish
ca. 1840
96 x 96 x 191/4 in.

"I move out my great cupboard for the accomodation of a closet behind," wrote Brother Henry DeWitt in his journal on March 7, 1846. Based on the entry, this cupboard over drawers has long been associated with Brother Henry (1805–1855). Until a few years ago, this handsome piece was built into a corner of a work-room in the Brethrens' workshop of the Church Family. The cupboard was positioned with its right end against one wall, and the back stood about three feet from the adjacent wall, which left a space behind it. The cupboard was then made into a walk-in closet by adding a door and a wide board to enclose the open end and by installing shelving against the wall on the other. A wide, ogee cornice molding was placed at the top over the original quarter-round cornice to fill the gap between cupboard and ceiling.

The design of the case combines a grid pattern, with twenty-four graduated drawers under four tall, slender two-panel doors. On the central wide stile of the case is stamped a ruler that measures from 3 to 6 1/2 feet. A height chart with a similar scale (cat. no. 81) lists the names of many Brothers and Sisters next to it, thus indicating their height.

Brother Henry Dewitt is better known as a "mechanic" rather than as a joiner, although he did chronicle numerous pieces of furniture that he built. On May 24, 1848, Brother Henry referred to finishing a drop-leaf table when he noted in his journal, "I put legs to a couple of table leafs at [the] washouse & hung them." Two years later, on February 1, 1850, he recorded that he had "made a counter 8 feet long with seven drawers on it and 2 cupboards."

Inside the right-hand portion of the cupboard, written in blue crayon, is the mysterious note, "First Snow / Oct 23 1889."

5
Cupboard over drawers

Pine, poplar, barium yellow,
red lead, chrome yellow, and
iron earth pigments, varnish
ca. 1850
68 1/2 x 48 3/4 x 18 7/8 in.

This classic cupboard over case of drawers is a showcase of design details common to Mount Lebanon Shaker furniture. Design characteristics shared by Mount Lebanon cabinetmakers abound, from the top of the case with its bull-nose-shaped cornice, to the rounded midrail and the straight, diagonally shaped cut foot. A rather refined miter joint was incorporated into the piece to join the cut foot with the bottom rail. This detail is found in several other case pieces and blanket boxes that are known to have been made at Mount Lebanon.

The drawer faces are finished with a simple, unlipped rounded edge, which, when closed, protrudes just beyond the face of the case. Many such case pieces are divided visually into top and bottom sections by the use of a distinctive yet simple rounded midcase molding as is found here, shaped on each end with a lamb's-tongue form. In a unique way this molding extends beyond the case sides. Also uncommon are the proportionally shorter doors, which give the case an unusual height of 68 1/2 inches.

The original salmon-colored pigment, now beneath a later varnish, was probably used by the craftsman as a wash to provide a distinctive color and to allow the figure and variation of the pine to show through. Though this classical form originated before the 1820s, the brass turn latches that secure the cupboard doors date this particular case piece to around 1850.

6
Cupboard over drawers

Pine, poplar, hardwood pulls,
yellow wash, varnish
ca. 1840
75 x 81 1/2 x 23 in.

Despite the classic use of the cupboard-over-drawers form, this massive case piece exhibits some unusual construction and design features. For example, the frame-and-panel construction of the case ends and the panels in the space flanking and between the cupboard doors is uncommon. (Case ends and stiles surrounding doors are frequently of simple plank construction.) This construction incorporates another rare feature: the case's combination of dovetailing with paneled-end construction. Only the stiles are dovetailed, which secures them into the top and bottom of the case. This distinctive construction technique is found in several pieces of furniture in the Mount Lebanon Shaker Collection (see appendix, nos. 1, 3) and may permit attribution to one particular furnituremaker or at least to one of the many active workshops.

Unidentified photographer, 1903
This cupboard over drawers is seen behind the Shaker Sisters who work in their sewing room at Mount Lebanon.

72

7

Cupboard and drawers

Ash, poplar, iron hinges and latches,
lock, porcelain knobs
Attributed to Austin E. Gage
1877
65 1/2 x 52 x 22 1/2 in.

"There have been 17 cases of drawers and cupboards, made in Pittsfield for Brethrens use, have been received into the new house": this journal entry dated March 7, 1877, as do several other entries, documents the construction and use of case pieces made of ash in the new Church Family dwelling. Outside help, such as that enlisted from furni-turemakers in Pittsfield, Massa-chusetts, and Albany, New York, was necessary after a massive fire at Mount Lebanon destroyed eight buildings and their contents in 1875. Among the vast quantities of furniture commissioned by the Family were cases of drawers, round and oval tables, marble-topped trestle tables, and beds. The large scale of the necessary rebuilding, the declining numbers of members at Mount Lebanon, and the advancing ages of the Brothers forced the Shakers to contradict their own counsel as described in the Millennial Laws:

"It is advisable for the center fami lies in each bishopric, to avoid hir-ing the world to make household furniture, except for the outer court." Although this cupboard and drawers was built by non-Shakers late in the nineteenth century, the form, specific design details, and concept of "plain and simple" are clearly intact in this commissioned piece of furniture.

Postcard, unidentified photographer, ca. 1895 (detail)
Corina Bishop (1843–1929) and an unidentified girl pose in a new Shaker dwelling built around 1877. The influence of the Victorian era is evident in the room's cluttered appearance. A case of drawers with porcelain knobs similar to those on this cupboard is seen in the background.

8
Cupboard with drawers and
tool brackets

Pine, basswood, fruitwood knobs, iron
hinges, brass latch, zinc yellow and iron
earth pigments, tempera paint
ca. 1840
94 3/4 x 73 1/8 x 9 7/8 in.

In addition to several work benches, this cupboard may be the most significant piece of work furniture constructed by Shaker cabinetmakers. Its overall size, asymmetrical layout, arrangement of doors, and use of color are all unusual. The massive cupboard stands over ninety-four inches tall, but it is under ten inches deep.

Apparently it was intended to be a tool cupboard, for many, although not all, of the tool holders were installed before the interior yellow paint was applied. Many of the tools can be reached through either of the two large doors. Yet even with these open, two other small doors in the case interior

must be opened to allow access to all the tools. To use space efficiently, tool brackets were affixed to the inside of the doors. Over time this caused the doors to sag considerably under the weight of the tools.

The large left-hand door is fitted with a lock, which when opened provides access to a forged iron latch that releases the right-hand door. For security, pins can be inserted through the case framework above or beside each drawer. The lack of paint on the right side of the case and the cornice molding there indicate that this piece was originally built into a corner.

Brother Henry DeWitt noted his construction of a tool cupboard in several entries of his journal.

July 19, 1837
I collected some stuff or boards for a tool cupboard. . . .

July 26, 1837
I made a cupboard to keep my tools in for jointering &c.

July 27, 1837
. . . finished the inside of said cupboard for hanging tools of various kinds.

It is interesting to speculate whether Brother Henry built and used this particular cupboard. The journal date of 1837 and the availability of yellow pigments at that time make this a reasonable possibility.

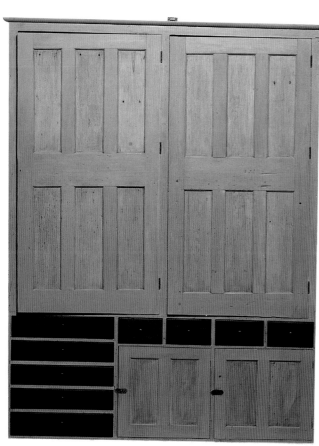

9
Case of drawers

Pine, basswood, fruitwood pulls,
zinc yellow, raw sienna, and
burnt sienna pigments, varnish
ca. 1830
74 3/4 x 48 x 23 5/8 in.

With virtually no decorative details other than a simple cut foot and a minimal square-edged cornice, this case is almost a step beyond the classically restrained but sparsely decorated "plain and simple" case piece. Its combination of three pigments—zinc yellow, raw sienna, and burnt sienna— and an oil binder provide a transparent but colored finish that was commonly applied on case pieces after 1830.

The case, which has an unusual depth of 24 inches, is lightened visually by the addition of small, diagonally shaped cut feet and two strings of cherry knobs. The knobs on the one-half-width drawers are placed ever so slightly off center so they continue the visual straight line created by the knobs on the full-width drawers. Interestingly, only one drawer is fitted with a lock, but it is not a top drawer, which is traditionally the one secured with a lock and key.

10
Cupboard

Pine, iron hinges, red ochre,
iron oxide red, lampblack, and
charcoal black pigments
ca. 1800
44 x 36 x 14 1/2 in.

This primitively made cupboard is characteristic of vernacular eighteenth-century construction. Early hand-forged nails and H-hinges, and opaque red paint are retained on the plank door. Despite its long existence at Mount Lebanon, no information describes its use or construction by a particular Shaker craftsman.

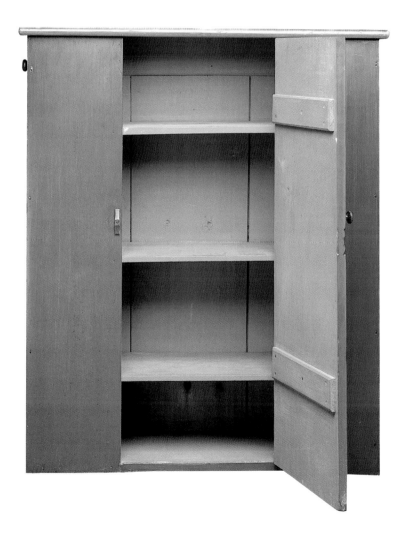

11

Cupboard

Butternut, pine, brass hinges,
glass, brown stain, shellac
Attributed to Orren Haskins
(1815–1892)
Inscribed in pencil: Feb. 1890 OH
No. 11
ca. 1880
36 3/4 x 24 1/4 x 10 1/8 in.

Although the inscription does not necessarily verify the maker of this cupboard, it is likely one of the many pieces made by Brother Orren Haskins. Built primarily of butternut, this small hanging cupboard is of frame-and-panel construction with unusual through-tenons exposed on the narrow face of the frame. The case sides, top, and bottom are rabbeted to expose a thin frame outside the door. A decorative bead was cut on the exposed case sides and on the inside of the vertical back-boards. The cupboard was obviously intended to be hung on the wall: the rear frame stiles were carefully notched to fit around a peg rail, and the back of the case was boxed to cover the rail.

A similar cupboard, inscribed "April 2, 1857," also exists in the Mount Lebanon Shaker Collection (see lower right). Signed on the back in pencil is "O. Haskins" and the inscription "Repaired Sep 1889." It deceptively appears to be of frame-and-panel construction, but it is actually a solid case with molding applied to resemble the stiles and rails of the case frame. Both are made of butternut, have glass rather than wood panel doors, and contain relatively thin shelves. These cupboards may have been constructed to store hymnals, but this particular use is uncertain.

12
Counter

Pine, fruitwood knobs, iron hinges,
red ochre pigment, varnish
ca. 1820
30 1/8 x 96 1/4 x 22 in.

The arrangement and small size of the two pairs of doors flanking the central banks of drawers are at present unknown on other Shaker counters. Also quite rare is the craftsman's use of dovetails in the construction of the pine case. Most Shaker craftsmen simply nailed the case sides to the top and bottom. This dovetail construction produced a different look that eliminated the substantial top overhang that is notable on so many pieces of Shaker storage and work furniture. Typical of the early case pieces and chairs is the opaque finish. Laboratory analysis indicates that the use of red ochre as the primary pigment created the counter's strong red color. The pigment was probably placed in an oil binder, which resulted in the depth of color evident in this piece.

13

Counter

Pine, cherry, butternut, basswood, fruitwood knobs, burnt sienna pigment, varnish
Made by Benjamin Lyon (1780–1870) and Charles Weed (1831–after 1862)

Written in pencil on drawer bottom: made Feby 1860 by Benjamin Lyon and Charles Weed 1860
33 1/2 x 79 1/4 x 35 3/4 in.

"Benjamin Lyon and Charles Weed are making a table with two rows of drawers for Hannah Train" concludes an entry dated March 1, 1860, in the farm journal kept at the "2nd order of the Church Family." The reference to a table implies the object's use as a work surface, most likely for the tailoring trade. Numerous references are made to the furniture that was employed by the Brothers and Sisters who made the Believers' clothing. In 1841 it was reported that Brother Isaac N. Youngs "about the middle of this month finished a job of work which he has been doing since the

7th of December for the Tailoresses ves. making two counters with drawers to them. The Tailoresses new shop is now pretty well finished and accomodations & they are well pleased with it" (New York State Library, Shaker Collection, Albany, 13500).

Two existing journals written by Brother Benjamin enumerate his many projects as a cabinetmaker. These two journals, written about fifteen and forty years before the construction of this counter, list a dining table, bedstead, case of drawers for the Brethrens' chamber, a chest for the Deacons, a

shop cupboard, many benches, and several other cupboards. Brother Benjamin was clearly a cabinetmaker of long standing at Mount Lebanon, and his career spanned more than forty years. He may have been one of the craftsmen who were crucial to forming and sustaining the Shaker style as we know it.

14
Counter

Pine, yellow poplar, cherry knobs,
varnish
ca. 1840
28 1/4 x 48 x 17 1/2 in.

Unusual features of this counter are its small size and the unique opening in its right side. Constructed of uncommonly heavy pine stock of about one inch in thickness, the case is quite strong for its size. In addition to the heavy sides, rails, and top, the case is further strengthened by two stretchers that extend the full length of the case and support the top and secure the case sides with dovetail joints that are visible on each end. The asymmetrical design is balanced by the four drawers that are placed opposite the rectangular opening. The absence of a fitted door is unusual and was possibly done to allow easy access to the tools, materials, bucket, or box that may have been stored inside.

15
Counter

Butternut, pine, fruitwood knobs,
chrome yellow, red ochre, red lead,
burnt sienna, and charcoal black
pigments, shellac, varnish

Attributed to Amos Stewart
(1802–1884)
ca. 1860
35 x 69 x 38 in.

Fitting well within the stylistic range of signed furniture constructed by Brother Amos Stewart, this counter is nearly identical to another that was built by this prolific cabinetmaker. This eight-drawer counter incorporates several features that are related to case furniture attributed to Brother Amos, such as the small half-housed dovetail on the drawer rail to frame the joint, the primary use of butternut, and the distinctive and identifiable large scrawling handwriting that indicates the location of drawers within the case. All members of the framework are of flat stock. Rather than use square stock for the corner posts, Brother Amos chose to employ flat stock that is about one-inch thick, which necessitated the addition of a diagonally sawn piece to complete the cut foot.

The shallow top drawers are unusual. The three cleats located just outside the case and centrally under the top not only help keep the broad top flat but also provide a way to secure the top to the base.

A similiar counter in a private collection is inscribed "AS 1873." Constructed of cherry with pine panels, it has only seven drawers: two banks of three half-width drawers, and a bottom drawer that extends the full width of the case rather than being divided into two half-width drawers.

16
Counter

Pine, yellow poplar, fruitwood knobs,
iron hinges, yellow wash, brown stain,
varnish
ca. 1830, altered ca. 1860
36 x 72 x 32 3/4 in.

In the Mount Lebanon Shaker Collection are two nearly identical eight-drawer pine counters (see appendix, no. 2). Both have graduated drawer heights of 4, 5, 6, and 8 3/4 inches, but with a 1-inch difference in case lengths.

Unlike the other counter, however, this one has an interesting construction or adaptation history. Above the original eight-drawer case a 4-inch high, dovetailed frame was fitted, and a half-round molding was added to conceal the joint. This framework was constructed to house four pull-out, drop-leaf supports. A drop leaf was then hinged to each end of the original top, which expanded the work surface considerably.

The craftsman used a construction technique common to a number of pieces built at Mount Lebanon (see cat. nos. 2, 14). For example, a stretcher about 1 by 2 inches in size was dovetailed into the front, rear, and center of the case sides to reinforce the large case. On some of these case pieces the dovetail itself is visible on the outside of the case.

17
Desk

Butternut, pine, iron pulls, varnish
Made by Amos Stewart (1802–1884)
Inscribed in pencil on two drawer
bottoms: March 1868 A S
1868
30 1/4 x 48 x 24 in.

The boldly penciled inscription "March 1868 A S" is located on the bottom of two drawers of this butternut and pine kneehole desk. The initials "A S" are those of Amos Stewart, a fine and prolific cabinetmaker at Mount Lebanon. At least eight known pieces of furniture are signed by him and are dated 1828, 1830, 1831, 1868, 1870, 1873, 1877, and 1878. Several other pieces, though unsigned and undated, can securely be attributed to him. His earliest known works are cupboard over drawers case pieces designed in a classic Shaker style.

In his later decades, however, Brother Amos seemed to favor frame-and-panel construction often with butternut as a primary wood, though he sometimes used a combination of woods in a single piece. In deviation from conventional practice, both in his choice of furniture design and materials, Brother Amos used cast-iron drawer pulls on this desk and on several other pieces that are now in private collections.

Brother Amos, along with Brothers Orren Haskins and Elisha Blakeman, are among a significant group of second-generation craftsmen who learned their trades as Shakers. Consequently, they introduced fewer outside influences into their furniture designs than had craftsmen who were already trained in the world before they joined the Shakers. Brother Amos was brought to Mount Lebanon when he was nine years old. By the age of twenty-four he had become an Elder, an important position he held for most of his life. His temporal activities were those of a "mechanic," and he worked as a joiner and furniture-maker for over sixty years.

18
Desk

Chestnut, cherry, pine, iron hinges
Attributed to Isaac N. Youngs
(1793–1865)
ca. 1840
29 1/2 x 23 3/4 x 19 1/2 in.

Originally made for use in the schoolhouse at Mount Lebanon, this desk was likely much longer than it is now. Rather than the single hinged top, it had four movable writing surfaces, with the desk originally being eight feet long. According to Jerry Grant in *Shaker Furniture Makers* (1989), one of these desks was discovered in the attic of the Church Family schoolhouse and purchased by collectors Faith and Edward Deming Andrews.

Brother Isaac was likely the maker of these desks, since he was extensively involved in the planning and construction of the schoolhouse in 1839. In a letter written to Elder Benjamin S. Youngs of South Union, Kentucky, Brother Isaac describes and provides measurements for a similar eight-foot-long desk. Such correspondence among Shaker craftsmen was fairly common and helped to ensure uniformity in design and construction throughout the widespread Shaker communities.

Unidentified photographer, ca. 1880
The long desks used in this girls' schoolroom
are attributed to Brother Isaac N. Youngs.

19
Tripod stand

Cherry, iron plate, varnish
ca. 1830
24 1/2 x 18 1/2 in. diameter

Representative of the best of "plain and simple" furniture, the design of this stand has been reduced to a simple curve that serves as its primary decorative element. The slender legs follow the snake leg form that was common in colonial New England, with the upper and lower surfaces of each leg being rounded and beveled, respectively. The thickness of each foot, about one-half inch, is uniform throughout its length. The craftsman incorporated a shallow concave curve into the design of the stem when he turned it, and he used a collar just below the cleat that secures the top. The stem is straight only where the legs are secured by sliding dovetails. A thin iron plate with screws reinforces the dovetail joint and reveals a construction feature common to most known stands from Mount Lebanon. A rounded edge completes the small table top. On the underside of the top a wood butterfly reinforcement was used to repair a crack.

Numerous tripod stands were used within the Believers' retiring rooms, halls, and work spaces whenever a small work stand was required or a table was needed to hold a candle or an oil lamp. The 1845 Millennial Laws provide that "one or two stands should be provided for the occupants of every retiring room." In the Church Family record titled "A Domestic Journal," Isaac N. Youngs notes in January 1837 that "David Rowley has undertaken to make a quantity of cherry tables, to furnish the great house, in the various rooms—has begun 20 tables." This might refer to a simple four-leg stand or to a tripod stand such as this.

20
Tripod stand with drawer

Cherry, pine, iron plate
ca. 1830
25 1/2 x 28 3/4 x 20 in.

Displaying the simple adaptation of the tripod stand form, the addition of the rectangular rimmed top and drawer creates a similar yet visually different piece of furniture. It could have been used as a small work table in one of the Sisters' shops or in an Eldress' retiring room.

This stand shows one of numerous adaptations of the tripod form. Here a solid case, constructed to surround and hold the drawer, was fastened on top of the doughnut-shaped disc. This disc is in turn affixed to the gracefully turned stem. The dovetailed drawer is accessible on only one side. On many Shaker stands, two drawers rather than one are found, and they are usually suspended under the top by two L-shaped brackets on which the drawer can be slid in or out. The drawers are commonly finished on both ends so they can be used from both sides of the stand.

21
Pedestal table

Walnut, yellow poplar, varnish
1877
28 1/2 x 44 x 38 in.

Uncommon in its oval shape, this varnished walnut table, along with numerous other similar pieces in the collection, was built for the "new" brick Church Family dwelling completed in 1877. These pedestal tables are unusual in the use of four rather than three legs, in their scale—they are notably larger than the more common tripod stand—and in the utilization of walnut instead of cherry wood. One or two drawers were affixed under several of the table tops, which raises the question of the tables' intended use. Two notations made in the "Domestic Occurrences" journal refer to them: on March 28, 1877, "Carpenters making round tables for [the] house"; and about a month later, "The round tables for Brethren's rooms are bro't into the house. . . ."

22
Work table

Pine, butternut, brass hinges, varnish
Attributed to Orren Haskins
(1815–1892)
Inscribed in pencil on drawer bottom:
9 February 1856 / Newspaper
apartment
1856
29 x 33 x 22 1/2 in.

23
Work table

Pine, oak, varnish
ca. 1850
27 1/4 x 35 3/4 x 16 in.

As one of many pieces altered by the Shakers to suit their needs, the inscription on this work table provides perhaps the only documentation for understanding the adaptation or use of this unusual table. Penciled in the handwriting style of Brother Orren Haskins are the words "9 February 1856 / Newspaper apartment," which indicates the table's use in the print shop or workroom. Not originally freestanding, the table has a dovetailed rectangular case with two drawers and was probably used on a table or counter. At a later date the tapered butternut legs were added to the case, which was built with considerably more skill. The top was originally secured to the case, but evidently it was later cut and hinged to provide access from the top.

More than utility was considered in the turning of the legs of this simple work bench. The turner combined two simple concave shapes divided by a swell, with three scribe lines separating the top and bottom sections of the leg. The top of the leg is somewhat enlarged just below the tenon, which is fitted into a hole drilled into the cleat that in turn supports the plain, rectangular plank top. The angle of the leg not only enhanced the design but also increased stability.

Precisely how this bench was used is not known. Its height suggests that it was employed with another bench to support a removable top or to hold boards or other light materials in a workshop setting. A similar though far simpler piece exists in the collection of the Shaker Museum and is marked "DR" for David Rowley. It was likely used as a saw horse by Brother David, who for many years worked as a carpenter and cabinetmaker for the North and Church Families at Mount Lebanon.

24
Bed

Maple, iron bolts, rope,
chrome green pigment
ca. 1830
33 x 76 x 32 in.

"Bedsteads should be painted green,—comfortables should be a modest color, not checked, striped or flowered," so states the Millennial Laws as they were revised in October 1845.

Imagine the color in a Shaker dwelling with retiring rooms arranged one after another down the hall, each with three or four green beds, several straight-back chairs and possibly a rocker, a cherry candle stand, and a red or yellow tall case of drawers, all set against white plastered walls. When the furniture was new, the colors were more brilliant and the finish more glossy than they are now.

This bed was once wider since it was built to hold two Brothers or Sisters. As the Shaker population declined, many large beds were cut down in width to accommodate one person. Evidence of this reduction in size is found in the inexact contour of the headboard, the shortened rails, and the disturbed finish. Numerous journal notations made after 1860 also refer to the use of single beds. Most were fitted with metal castings and wooden wheels, which allowed for easy movement when making the beds or cleaning under them.

25
Meetinghouse bench

Pine, stain, varnish
1824
27 1/2 x 133 x 14 in.

This simple bench was built into the west side of the meetinghouse at Mount Lebanon in 1824. The plank seats with plain backs were intended for the observers who attended the Shakers' worship services. Such benches stood in place until around 1960, when the meetinghouse was renovated for use as a library.

Unidentified photographer, ca. 1940
Tiered rows of benches, intended for worldly visitors, line the west wall of the second meetinghouse, which was built in 1824.

26
Meetingroom bench

Walnut, plywood, brass upholstery
nails, varnish
ca. 1880
34 x 72 1/2 x 19 in.

Standing in stark contrast to the plain benches installed in 1824 (cat. no. 25) are the fancy, mass-produced benches manufactured by Gardner & Co. and used in the Church Family's winter meetingrooms. An advertisement in the New York *Christian Advocate* for Thursday, July 3, 1884, claimed that these perforated benches "do not heat the body, will not fade, collect dust, nor get eaten up by moths, as is the case with cushioned seats." Brass upholstery nails fasten the bent plywood seats to a walnut frame of Victorian design. The installation of these benches, padded with cushions, in the Church Family dwelling clearly indicates the evolution of Shaker aesthetic sensibilities in the late 1870s. Was it caused by growing acceptance of worldly goods, or by a more progressive interest in contemporary taste and a desire for comfort in living spaces? Many photographs taken in the closing decades of the nineteenth century show other commercial Victorian furniture being used in Shaker dwellings.

Photographed by William Winters, ca. 1930
The Church Family winter meetingroom in the new 1876 dwelling.

27

Side chair

Bird's-eye maple, brass tilters,
cane seat
Attributed to Brother
George O. Donnell
ca. 1850
37 x 18 1/2 x 14 1/2 in.

Built of decorative bird's-eye maple, this rare chair is an exceptional example of Mount Lebanon craftsmanship. It remains as one of about a dozen special cane-seated chairs with metal tilters that were likely made by Brother George O. Donnell. This side chair displays the brass tilters that Brother George patented in 1852 to prevent "the wear and tear of carpets and the marring of floors, caused by the back posts of chairs as they take their natural motion of rocking backward and forward." Wooden tilters were fitted on many Shaker chairs, but metal ones are far more uncommon.

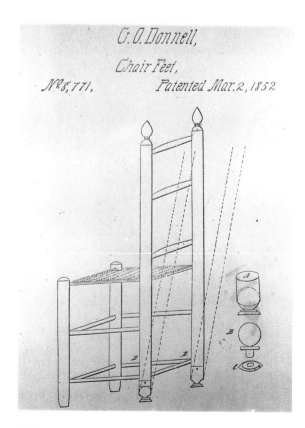

28
Rocking chair

Maple, bird's-eye maple, ash splint
Inscribed in ink on seat bottom:
Hannah Bryant
ca. 1840
44 x 21 1/4 x 22 1/4 in.

Typical of Shaker rockers made by
the 1840s, this example incorporates shaped side-scroll arms,
straight backposts with simple
turned pommels, tapered front
posts with a small collar turned just
beneath the arm, and thin rocker
blades inserted into slots. This
rocker stands out for two reasons:
the craftsman's choice of decorative bird's-eye maple is unusual;
and the chair retains what is probably its original ash splint seat,
which is signed "Hannah Bryant."

29
Chair catalogues

Letterpress ink on paper
ca. 1880
5 3/4 x 3 1/4, 5 x 3 in.

30
Chair broadside

Ink on paper
ca. 1930
5 x 3 1/2 in.

Broadsides served the Shakers as an initial form of advertising their production of chairs. Styles and prices were simply listed on single sheets of paper. Illustrations of chairs appeared on the second variation of the broadside. The earliest known Shaker chair catalogue is dated 1874, and more than a dozen illustrated editions were printed over the years. Not until the publication of the catalogues were chairs assigned numbers from 0 through 7, progressing from the smallest to the largest in the line.

In 1863 Brother Robert Wagan (1833–1883) assumed the duties of deacon in the newly formed South Family. He had previously worked in and then managed the chair production of the Second Family. Under his guidance and marketing abilities, however, the South Family's chair industry reached a national level. Elder Henry Blinn, from the Shaker community at Canterbury, New Hampshire, visited Mount Lebanon in 1872 and recorded his observations about the chair factory and Brother Robert.

One of the most singular things connected with this is, that a few years ago they made a small business in making and selling chairs, but never considered it of much importance, till it passed into the hands of the present manager. He enlarged the business and the demand has increased correspondingly. Br. Robert is enterprising. He says anything will sell that is carried into the

market. . . . The building erected last year, & the machinery in it has cost some $25,000. . . . They have an engine of 15 horsepower and a boiler of 20 horsepower. The whole building is heated by steam. Some ten hands are employed, & it is expected that they will finish two doz. chairs per day. . . . Already they have orders for more than they can furnish. . . .

A new line of chairs was developed, which marked the standard for Shaker design for more than fifty years. What influenced the change is not clear. Was it caused by new machinery and the introduction of mass-production techniques, or did the Shakers now choose to cater to the perceived preferences of a worldly market?

This small broadside promoting chairs is among the last of the known Shaker chair advertisements. It appeared in a local periodical or pamphlet around 1930, near the end of the Shakers' 150-year history of manufacturing chairs. By the early twentieth century the chair industry was operated by a handful of Shakers and outside help who hired out most aspects of the chairs' construction. The chairs appear somewhat less refined than those produced twenty-five to fifty years earlier.

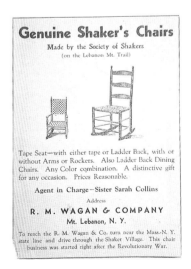

31
Rocking chair

Maple, wool tape, logwood stain,
shellac
Stamped: 1
Decal on inside of rocker blade
ca. 1880
29 1/8 x 16 1/2 x 19 5/8 in.

32
Rocking chair

Maple, wool tape, cotton ticking, logwood stain, shellac
Stamped: 3
Decal on bottom slat
ca. 1880
33 1/4 x 21 x 24 7/8 in.

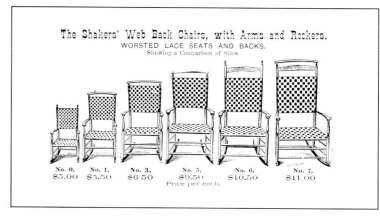

33
Rocking chair

Maple, cloth tape, upholstery,
logwood stain, shellac
Stamped: 7
ca. 1890
41 x 25 1/4 x 31 in.

These chairs, stamped with the
numbers 1, 3, and 7, are part of
the line of furniture that the
Shakers marketed in their own
showrooms, through catalogue
sales (see below), and through
retail establishments nationwide.
Often distinguished with a gold
decal, these chairs displayed similar
design features:

• Gently bent back posts with
  acorn-shaped pommels or a
  cushion rail
• Steam-bent arched back slats
  or a cloth-taped back
• Vase-shaped front posts
• Thin rocker blades slotted into
  the posts
• Crescent-shaped arms with two
  projections where the wrist and
  elbow would rest
• Upholstered frames or a wide
  variety of wool-taped seats, with
  or without optional upholstered
  cushions

34
Fabrics

Cotton, wool, metallic-wrapped
thread
ca. 1830–1850
39 x 71 in. (average)

Until the end of the nineteenth century, much of the Shakers' clothing was made by Brothers and Sisters who practiced tailoring. Many Shaker communities also raised their own sheep for wool and grew flax for linen as well. The plant stalks were retted or rotted, worked on a flax brake, and hackled, separated, and straightened. The finer fibers were used for linen cloth, the coarser for sacking materials or rope. Those communities that grew mulberry trees to feed silk worms were able to produce silk fabrics. Fine color silk kerchiefs were laboriously made on Shaker looms. By the mid-nineteenth century, however, Family account books began to record the purchase of ready-made fabrics, which eliminated the lengthy and often tedious steps required to process materials.

Although specific colors or types of fabrics were used for special occasions, such as blues and grays for worship garments, Shaker clothing varied widely over the years. This fine cloth is merely a sampling of the range of colors and materials used. Their plain appearance belie their complex construction, with dyed threads of cotton and wool woven together to produce vibrant colors. Recipe books for dyeing fabrics and extant garments suggest the Shakers enjoyed an abundant variety of colors, from lavender, purple, slate, and gray, through a range of reds, oranges, rusts, and browns.

35
Loom

Birch, maple, iron
Inscribed by Sadie Neale and
E. Bierge
ca. 1850
70 1/2 x 27 7/8 x 49 1/2 in.

Looms, such as this small Shaker-made one, were employed by the Sisters most likely to weave poplar cloth, a component in the poplar-ware industry. Poplarware was a unique product not made outside the Shakers' communities. The unusual cloth was woven with the warp of the loom prepared with cotton thread. Into the weft,

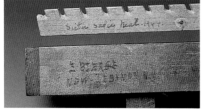

Sister Mary Hazard (1811–1899)
works at her loom.

however, thin strips of poplar were woven to create an unusual fabric that combined wood and thread. Since the resulting cloth had little integral strength, it was glued or sewn to a backing of cloth, wood, or cardboard, depending on its ultimate use.

A cardboard form and a wooden base provided the structure for the various shapes of poplarware boxes. The poplar cloth was attached to a cardboard form and then trimmed with fine leather. A similarly finished lid was added with hinges of colorful ribbons. A pin cushion, needle case, ball of wax, or a small amount of emery was often secured to the box with ribbons. In the late nineteenth and early twentieth centuries, fancy poplarware sewing boxes were among the staples sold in Shaker display rooms, along with brush baskets, oval boxes, and postcards of the Believers and their communities.

36
Dress

Cotton, silk, glass buttons
Collar: cotton warp, wool weft
ca. 1870
53 in. long

Brothers and Sisters alike were involved in the ongoing tasks of making clothing by hand for all those in the Shaker communities. Men served as tailors for the Brethren, while women sewed for themselves. Cloth was also woven by hand until the mid-nineteenth century, when it was deemed more economical to purchase material. Apprenticeships for new or younger Believers not only offered direct experience with sewing but also supplied additional hands for producing the vast quantities of clothing that were needed by the community.

Long counters (see cat. nos. 12–14) provided work space for the tailors and tailoresses. Smaller sewing tables or desks were employed for hand work and mending. The wide range of work furniture, with the nearly endless variations of sizes, arrangements of drawers and cupboards, and placement of drop leafs, attests to the importance of the tailoring trade within the United Society. Like many others in "the World," Shakers welcomed the introduction of foot-powered sewing machines in the 1860s. Comments in Shaker journals describe the eagerness with which sewing machines were put into use, and notations were made regarding the purchase or benefits of particular brands.

Despite the uniform appearance of their clothing, tailors and tailoresses among the Shakers devised patterns to fit the needs and shapes of individual Believers. They also created several complex systems to assist in the fashioning of apparel. Brother Hervey Eads, of Union Village, Ohio, developed the "Tailor's System for Cutting Shakers' Garments." Another guide likely used at Mount Lebanon was the "Dressmaker's Magick Scale," which provided instructions on cutting the Sisters' gowns and fitting garment pieces.

Photograph by J.E. West, ca. 1885
Eldress Catherine Allen (ca. 1850–1922) was instrumental in having the Western Reserve Historical Society in Cleveland, Ohio, preserve its vast collection of Shaker documents.

37
Bonnet

38
Bonnet

Silk, silk chenille, silk velvet,
wool batting
ca. 1850
8 x 12 x 9 in. (each)

For much of the nineteenth century, bonnets were a basic part of the dress of Shaker Sisters. Beverly Gordon in *Shaker Textile Arts* (1980) notes the importance of wearing a bonnet as a rite of passage and quotes a Sister who remembered, "My friend Joy and I were each fifteen years of age when we were removed from the children's order and became young sisters. . . . A fresh palm leaf bonnet with a swiss muslin curtain and a worsted 'meeting gown' made the summit of our bliss" ("Fifteen Years a Shakeress," *The Galaxy* [January-April 1872]).

Changes in form, materials, and colors can be seen in the stylistic development of bonnets as well as in other Shaker clothing. These particular bonnets probably date from the mid-nineteenth century. Toward the end of the century, the enforcement of rules stressing uniformity relaxed considerably, and Shaker Sisters began wearing simple, sheer "caps" rather than bonnets.

39

Cloak

Wool, silk
ca. 1880–1930
61 in. long

During her exceptionally long life as a
Shaker, Emma Neale was closely associated
with many aspects of the Mount Lebanon
community, including its well-known
line of cloaks.

An advertisement in the Shaker
sales catalogue *Products of
Intelligence and Diligence* (cat.
no. 40) states that "making the
SHAKER CLOAK, which is an
unique and comfortable garment,
is one of the principal industries
carried on at the present time,
and commands large patronage."
Cloaks were available in many bold
colors, including "Navy blue,
Harvard red, and Dartmouth
green." An additional four-page
sales brochure published at Mount
Lebanon marketed the popular
cloak under the name of Emma J.
Neale and Company. Eldress
Emma Neale (1847–1943) received
a trademark for the cloak in 1901.

These finely sewn and flowing
wool garments were indeed popular. Mrs. Grover Cleveland ordered
one in dove gray to wear to her
husband's second presidential
inauguration in 1893. The cloak
is probably best known as a
"Dorothy Cloak," named in honor
of its original designer, Sister
Dorothy Durgin of Canterbury,
New Hampshire.

Unidentified photographer, ca. 1880
The Sisters' sewing room at
Mount Lebanon

Paper, ink
ca. 1900
7 x 4 5/8 in.

Throughout the nineteenth century, the economic base of northeastern states shifted from largely agriculture to industry. The Shakers were forced to evolve as well, particularly due to changing demographics within their communities. Profits from agriculture substantially decreased and comprised a smaller percentage of community income. This loss was supplemented, in part, by the extensive line of fancy goods produced by the Sisters.

The small, illustrated catalogue *Products of Intelligence and Diligence* was directed toward the growing tourist trade.

Featured products—some useful, others simply souvenirs—were targeted primarily for ladies traveling to Mount Lebanon or through that area of New York state. Sewing paraphernalia, oval carriers, spool stands, work bags, daisy emerys, and melon cushions were illustrated, along with Shaker cloaks, poplarware boxes, and dolls.

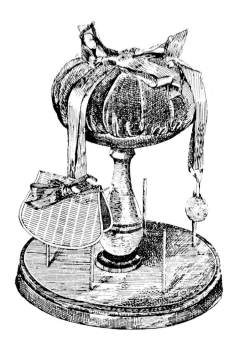

Numerous Shaker-made goods were advertised in the *Products of Intelligence and Diligence*. Among them are this sewing carrier and spool stand, which are similar to those seen in cat. nos. 42 and 43.

Mount Lebanon, N. Y., _____ 1874

Friend _____

Bought of _____

DEALERS IN

Baskets, Fans, Spool Tables, Cushions, and a variety of Fancy Articles.

STORE OPPOSITE THE CHURCH.

Unidentified photographer, ca. 1880
Mary Hazard (1811–1899), Floradia Sears (1825–1901), and Amelia Calver (1843–1929) sell goods in the Shaker store at Mount Lebanon. This receipt, dated 1874, shows the variety of products that were sold by the Shakers.

41
Doll

Porcelain, leather, cotton,
wool, silk, poplarware bonnet
ca. 1920
15 1/2 in. long

Illustrated in *Products of Intelligence and Diligence,* such dolls differed from most Shaker products. Many were sold in their stores in the early twentieth century and were presented as gifts by some of the Sisters. Commercially made doll bodies were purchased and then carefully clothed in garments that replicated the Sisters' own style of dress. The Sisters probably used scrap materials found in their sewing rooms. For example, the material of the doll's cloak appears to be identical to that of some of the full-sized cloaks. Complete outfits were made for the dolls, from the undergarments to the wool dress and cloak, and including the palm leaf bonnet under the cloak hood. This particular doll has a fine French porcelain head marked "Armand Maruse" and a body made of leather and cloth.

42

Spool stand

Cherry, shellac, brass, green velvet, silk
ribbons, woven poplar, cotton threads
ca. 1900
6 1/4 x 5 3/4 in. diameter
4 1/4 in. diameter of cushion

"The good sisters led the way into
the shop, saying that they did not
keep it warmed in winter, so few
strangers came that way. We
entered the room, which was per-
fumed with extracts and woodwork. It was all in confusion; but
there were the nests of boxes, and
the delicate baskets, and the white
table-mats, and yellow silk-winders,
and the floor-mats and rocking-
chairs. . ." ("A Day Among the
Shakers," *Once a Week* [London],
May 24, 1862).

Products manufactured by the
Sisters provided a substantial source
of income for the Shakers. The
prominence of their stores in numerous photographs taken of Mount
Lebanon attest to their importance
in the community. Like many other
objects offered for sale, the wooden
parts of this spool stand as well as
the spools themselves were created
in a cooperative effort with the
Brothers or were hired out to
woodworkers beyond the Shaker
community. The Sisters made the
pin cushions.

43
Sewing carrier

Maple, pine, shellac, silk lining
Attributed to John Roberts
ca. 1930
4 5/8 x 12 x 8 1/4 in.

Hundreds of colorfully lined and outfitted sewing carriers were made for sale in the Shaker stores located on the Albany-Boston post road at Mount Lebanon. This particular carrier, which holds a pin cushion, needle sharpener, and thread wax, was originally lined in peach-colored silk. Others exist in bold red and shades of blue and green. It was likely made by John Roberts, a local resident who for years worked for the Shakers. He also manufactured a huge quantity of oval boxes, which are often identifiable due to his use of plywood for the box or carrier bottoms and his oversize copper or brass fasteners. Mr. Roberts also produced cherry candle stands, which were sold by the Shakers. *Products of Intelligence and Diligence* list three sizes of lined carriers priced from $2.50 to $5.00.

44
Rug

Wool, cotton, burlap
ca. 1850
24 1/2 x 43 in.

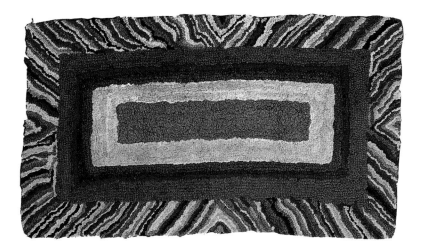

Capitalizing on the curiosity of outsiders, postcards and stereoscopic views of the Shakers and their community were created for the tourist trade. This studio photograph of Sister Sarah Collins, dating from November 1883, was sold as a postcard.

Decoration was increasingly accepted in the Believers' world as the nineteenth century drew to a close. It emerged in several ways: in the flexibility of garments, the mixing of woods in Shaker-made furniture, the purchase of commercially manufactured Victorian furniture, and the display of pictures, fancy calendars, and advertisements in their dwellings or workrooms. Rugs also added decoration and color to the Shakers' living spaces. Long runners protected stairways, small rugs graced entryways, and area rugs enlivened retiring rooms. Shaker rugs made of various materials, patterns, and processes, such as braiding, hooking, knitting, and weaving, differ little from those created in "the World."

Sister Sarah Collins, who came to Mount Lebanon as a child during the Civil War, was the last survivor of the South Family and was known for her skill at making rugs.

Several photographs from the 1930s and 1940s show her posed with some of her creations on display. In photographs of the Shakers' chair showrooms, rugs for sale are seen hanging on the walls behind rows of upholstered chairs. With rugs such as this, the Shakers attempted to appeal to the eclectic tastes of the Victorian era.

Since the form and process of this colorful hooked rug can be traced to the Shaker communities at both Mount Lebanon and Canterbury, New Hampshire, a definite attribution is impossible to make. Even so, the mix of colors and the rectangular design certainly brightened any space where the rug was used.

Pine, white and black paint
Written in pencil: John Lee
Dated: October 31, 1825
13 1/4 x 124 x 5/8 in.

With the appointment of Brother Seth Wells as the superintendent of all Shaker schools in 1832, the formal education of Shaker children was encouraged throughout the widespread communities. Such education was, however, largely directed toward learning practical skills and becoming valued members of the United Society. Children were separated from adults and raised under the guidance of "caretakers." Regulations in the Holy Orders of the Church (1844) legislated that "children belonging to the Church must be schooled by themselves, the boys in the winter and the girls in the summer, three or four months, according

lead. I say, and hear ye my word, Reading, writing, a small portion of Grammar, Arithmetic and Geography, with a very small portion of some religious histories work, are plenty sufficient for any child to learn. . . ."

The use of such alphabet boards as educational teaching aids is supported by a woodcut engraving, published in *Frank Leslie's Illustrated Newspaper* (September 6, 1873), that shows two of them hanging on the wall of a schoolhouse. Both sides of the boards were painted, with one displaying the alphabet in cursive letters, the other in block letters.

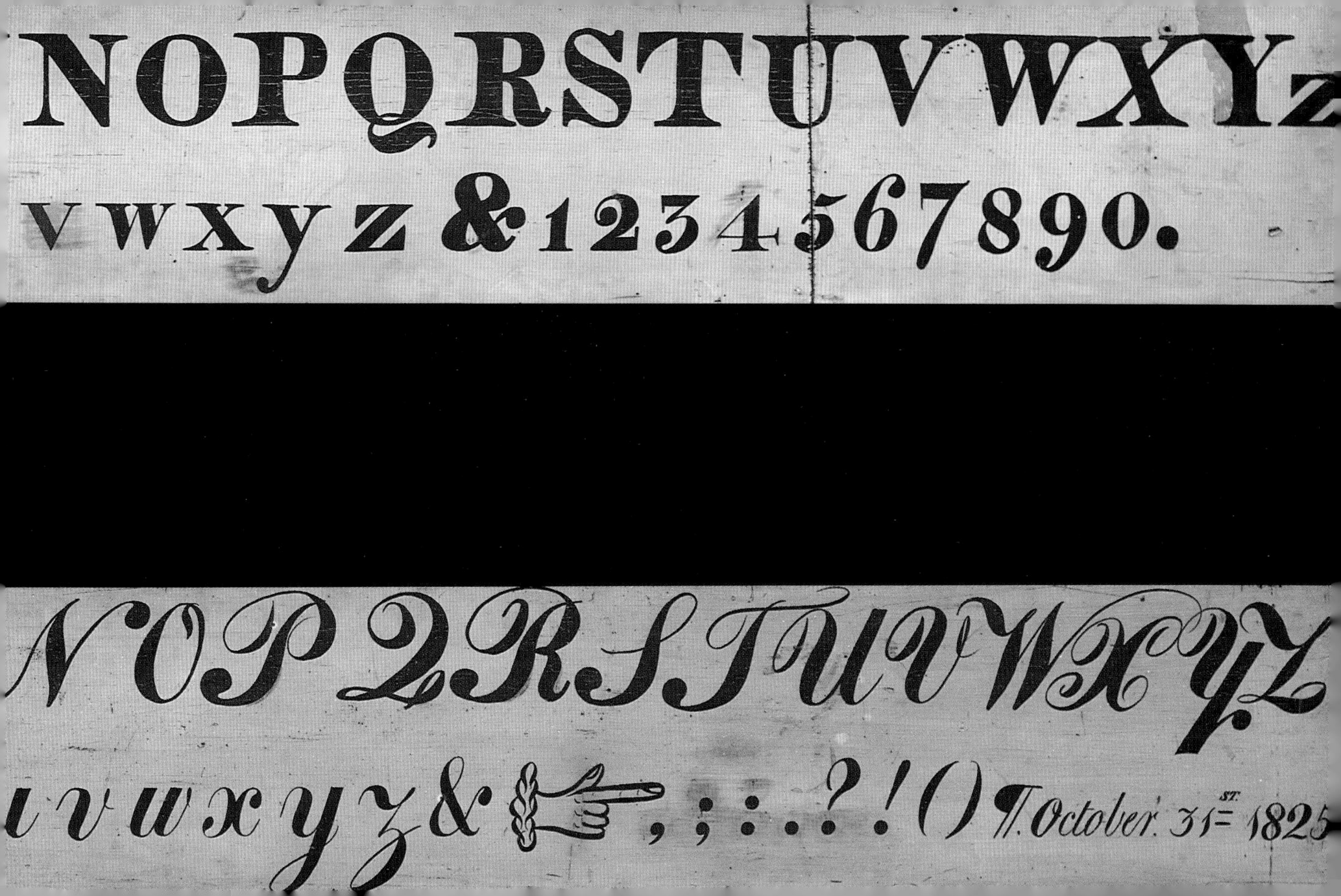

NOPQRSTUVWXYz

vwxyz & 1234567890.

NOPQRSTUVWXYZ

vwxyz & ☞ ,;:..?!()¶. *October 31st 1825*

46
Alphabet board

Pine, black and gold paint
ca. 1820
5 3/4 x 71 1/8 x 1/2 in.

The handwritings found in
Shaker journals, diaries, and
account books show the care
and precision with which
penmanship must have been
practiced in Shaker schools.

rfstuvwxyz.1234567890

47
Round storage boxes and measures

Maple, pine, copper tacks, varnish,
paint
ca. 1830–1880
No. 7: 3 x 4 1/2 in. diameter
No. 8: 3 1/4 x 6 in. diameter
No. 20: 3 1/2 x 7 1/4 in. diameter
Large box: 6 x 13 3/4 in. diameter

Different groups of skilled crafts-men and women within the com-munity, from makers of baskets and boxes to tinsmiths and carpenters, manufactured containers for stor-ing, measuring, and transporting goods. The largest of these con-tainers, with short, carefully cut fin-gers or swallowtails, as the Shakers called them, was of a variety crafted by those who made oval boxes. Small, malleable copper tacks secured the rim and the overlapping fingers. Its precise purpose is unknown, although other contain-ers that are somewhat shallower and larger in diameter were employed as spit boxes when tobacco was used in the communi-ty. The smaller boxes with numbers were utilized to measure dry prod-ucts, such as flour, seeds, or grain.

48

Oval box

Maple, pine, copper tacks and points,
red wash, shellac
ca. 1850
3 5/8 x 9 3/8 x 6 7/8 in.

A range of oval boxes were illustrated and advertised in the Shakers' chair catalogues. Sizes varied from #1 to #11, and other sizes could be made to meet particular needs. A stack of seven boxes was also available. For many years the quantities of boxes produced were listed by Brother Isaac N. Youngs in his year-end report in his "Domestic Journal." In 1836, for example, 3,560 boxes were manufactured. A total of 24,250 boxes was listed in previous years.

To make these widely recognized oval boxes, the maple sides were heated with steam or immersed in hot water until pliable, and then bent around a wooden form. The sides were placed on followers, which forced the wood to retain the oval shape until it dried. The swallowtails were carefully cut by hand with a knife and secured in place with copper tacks. An oval bottom was squeezed into the form and fastened with wood or brass points. A similarly constructed top was then fitted. To enliven the box's appearance, a wash of red ochre, mustard, or yellow was sometimes applied before a shellac or varnish finish sealed the surface.

Essential to the box making trade at Mount Lebanon were Brothers Daniel Boler and Daniel Crosman, who, along with other mechanics, developed specialized machinery that modernized the industry. Their efforts improved the critical process of cutting the elliptically shaped tops and bottoms, which had previously been done by hand. Because of the huge quantities of boxes manufactured each year, special tools and machines were developed that standardized the production process. The wooden sides, for example, were planed on a Daniels planer. A series of wooden forms and followers was devised for bending the wooden sides. Numbered tin patterns were used to lay out the swallowtail shapes quickly.

49
Basket

Ash
ca. 1840
13 1/2 x 21 1/2 in.

At their most utilitarian level, baskets were used to transport, sort, or store produce, laundry, and kindling. From our twentieth-century perspective and familiarity with plastic laundry baskets and cardboard boxes, the use of such fine basketry for everyday tasks might seem extravagant.

The Shakers took great care in selecting materials for baskets, which are usually made of black ash. To prepare the wood for baskets, an extensive system that involved a trip hammer and a variety of water-powered and hand tools was developed at Mount Lebanon. The trade became so specialized that several Brothers or Sisters were required to ready the wood for weaving, while others cut and shaped the fine handles. Still others did the weaving and attached the handles and rims as the baskets were assembled. Interestingly, many Elders and Eldresses in the ministry at Mount Lebanon were basketmakers.

50

Convenience chair

Pine, birch, iron, mustard yellow paint
ca. 1830
15 x 15 1/2 in. diameter

One visitor to Mount Lebanon noted of the Shakers,

The Scientific American, Journal of Chemistry, New York Tribune, Boston Herald, American Agriculturalist, and *The Sanitary Engineer* . . . are in their reading room. . . . It seems singular that a community whose main thoughts are turned toward spiritual things and to preparing for another life should be so zealous to secure bodily health. The results of this care and attention are shown in the remarkable vigor and longevity of all their members. . . . The Shaker doctrines as regards hygiene is simple, and included plain and wholesome food, manual labor for all, early and regular hours and good ventilation. The sanitary arrangements are well worth imitating. In each dwelling room there are baths, sinks, and w.c.'s, all well ventilated, while the out-door privies, which are more generally used, are treated much the same as earth closets, the material being taken away every few days and composted. . . . The elders (of the North Family)

informed me that their careful attention to hygiene has a theological basis, they believing that science and religion, "Truly so called," are one and the same (reprinted in *The Manifesto* 19 [May 1889]).

Of the many "convenience chairs" used throughout the Shaker community, few still exist. The Mount Lebanon origin of this one is suggested by its great similarity to another stamped "DM" for Brother David Meacham. This convenience chair, which held a ceramic pot inside, was more portable than many others that were used indoors in a more permanent setting. In the first volume of *Shaker Woodenware,* the suggestion is made that similar ones may have been used to "preserve the modesty of the Sisters who carried [the chair] to the field or garden for use when returning to the privy was inconvenient." The convenience chair itself retains a darkened mustard yellow paint with a varnish on the seat and lid portions.

This convenience chair was a product of the cooper's trade. Coopering, the making of barrels and pails, was practiced in most Shaker communities. Enfield and Canterbury, New Hampshire, were particularly well known for their extensive coopering industries.

51
Mirror stands

Cherry, basswood, birch
ca. 1840
24 x 14 x 2 in.
16 x 8 1/2 x 1 in.

The use of these mirrors may reflect a somewhat different spirit in the Shaker community, for Brothers and Sisters were not concerned with the fashion and vanity of "the World" but were instead interested in being neat and proper. The 1845 Millennial Laws specifically address the utilization of mirrors:

One good looking glass, which ought not to exceed eighteen inches in length, and twelve in width, with a plain frame. A looking glass larger than this, ought never to be purchased by Believers. If necessary a small glass may hang in the closet, and a very small one may be kept in the public cupboard of the room" (Millennial Laws, August 7, 1821; revised October 1845, sec. X, 3).

Most Shaker mirrors were housed in simply molded frames supported on inverted T-shaped holders that were hung on a nail or pegboard. Even this unpretentious household item showed the inevitable progression toward Victorian style. Gradually wider frames with veneer were used. Many had small pins or pegs in the ledge, which may have conveniently held brushes and combs.

52
Stepladder

Pine, varnish
ca. 1850
29 1/2 x 25 x 23 in.

Departing from pure function, craftsmen employed a simple curve to enhance the design of this small stepladder. Several ladders of this more-than-ordinary design can be found in a variety of sizes and colors. Small and light, such ladders were easily portable and provided quick access to the tops of tall cupboards and cases of drawers.

53
Copper dipper with iron handle

Forged copper, iron
ca. 1830
23 1/2 x 1 3/4 in.;
bowl 8 1/4 in. diameter

54
Iron dipper

Forged iron
ca. 1830
23 1/2 x 1 1/2 in.;
bowl 8 in. diameter

Account books kept by the Shakers chronicle the array of architectural and household articles that were made by blacksmiths at Mount Lebanon, including latches, door handles, hinges, knives, and forged kitchen utensils. Both dippers have skillfully but simply forged iron handles. The larger one is uncommon in that it incorporates a copper bowl, 8 1/4 inches in diameter. These utensils may well have been put to good use in one of the kitchens in which food was prepared three times daily for up to a hundred members in the larger Shaker Families.

An oversize Shaker kitchen, with its large stoves and ovens, and long tables for food preparation, differed quite radically from that in a typical New England household. Cooking pots had to hold gallons of soup, and ovens baked a dozen pies or several loaves of bread at one time. The floor plan of the North Family dwelling, as documented around 1940, shows a main kitchen with a massive cook stove. At least seven specialized food preparation areas or storerooms are noted, including a pantry, a second storeroom, a bake room, a bakers' buttery, a preserves buttery, a preserving kitchen, and a scullery. Three dining rooms were served. The largest, the general dining room for the North Family itself, was placed adjacent to two much smaller rooms in which visitors and farm help were fed.

55
Pitcher

Porcelain
1886–1887
7 3/4 x 8 1/4 x 4 in.

56
Plate

Porcelain
1886–1887
7 1/2 in. diameter

57
Bowl

Porcelain
1886–1887
2 1/2 x 5 1/2 in. diameter

"We have a set of new dishes on our table [this] morning, marked Shakers Mt Lebanon, they are pretty and costly we know," commented a Sister of the Church Family in her diary on February 20, 1887. Another Sister noted in her diary, "We have a surprise of great value, on our breakfast table; a set of new dishes. Porcelain ware marked for us Shakers &c. . . . we hope it may be long ere we need another set." According to Jerry Grant ("Collections Report," vol.1, no.1 [May 1990], Shaker Museum and Library,) the fine set of china was made on special order by the Union Porcelain Works of Greenpoint, New York, one of the few American-based porcelain manufacturers. It is not clear what kind of table service this china replaced, though it was most likely simple, unmarked porcelain. Similar dinnerware bearing the names of other Shaker communities is at present unknown. Other pieces from this set, including oval serving dishes, a round bowl, and dinner plates, are in the collection at the Shaker Museum and Library in Old Chatham, New York.

58
Dustpan

Tin-plated iron
ca. 1830–1880
9 x 9 1/8 x 1 3/4 in.

59
Broom

Hardwood broom handle,
broom corn
ca. 1830–1880
9 x 3 x 1 3/4 in.

Cleanliness, probably more than any other aspect of Shaker life, received regular comment from outside visitors. As one observed, "Great importance is attached to cleanliness; this luxury they appear to enjoy in a truly enviable degree."

Symbolic of the Shakers' interest in cleanliness is the ever-present tin dustpan, which was hung from a small peg in the kitchen or entry-way or on a woodbox. This dust-pan, purchased by Faith and Edward Deming Andrews from Mount Lebanon, is particularly well constructed, with a triangular rein-forcement where the handle meets the pan joint, the point of greatest strain. The gracefully curved sides are strengthened by a wire rolled into the edge and by the curve itself. The broad working edge of the pan was folded, helping it to lie flat and greatly increasing its strength. Documentation indicates the Shakers both produced such tinware in their own workshops and purchased it from peddlers.

Two innovations in the broom industry have been credited to the Shakers. One was a special screw-fed lathe for the rapid turning of broom handles. The other was the development of the flat broom. A clamp they devised held the broom stalks or fibers flat, which considerably broadened the func-tional width of the final broom and held it secure while it was sewn and attached to the handle.

The broom industry employed many Brothers in several communi-ties, including Mount Lebanon. Brother Isaac N. Youngs recorded in his year-end report for 1846 that "444 doz. & 8 brooms [were] made in the course of the year and 55 doz. small coarse corn brushes & made by Elisha Blakeman & Charles Lovegrove. About 109 doz. small fine corn brushes wound with brass wire, made by Philemon Stewart & 12 dozen by Benjamin Gates."

60
Stove

Cast and forged iron
ca. 1840
21 x 12 3/4 x 29 1/2 in.
(without stovepipe)

Stoves such as this were found in most rooms of Shaker dwellings and workspaces. Cast of iron and relatively airtight, these stoves were rather efficient. Some were even fitted with "super heaters," a cast rectangular fixture that was fitted atop the stove to help retain more heat in the room rather than sending it up the chimney.

Shaker craftsmen made several variations of wood patterns for use in the casting process. A certain amount of grinding and filing would have been necessary to clean up the casting and to fit the box tightly to its base. A blacksmith finished the stove by forging the draft and a latch for the door. Several references to foundry work done at Mount Lebanon appear in early journals, but in later years patterns were taken to area foundries.

61

Kindling box

Basswood, ash, brass, tin, iron, paint
ca. 1890
18 3/4 x 15 x 13 1/2 (with handle up)

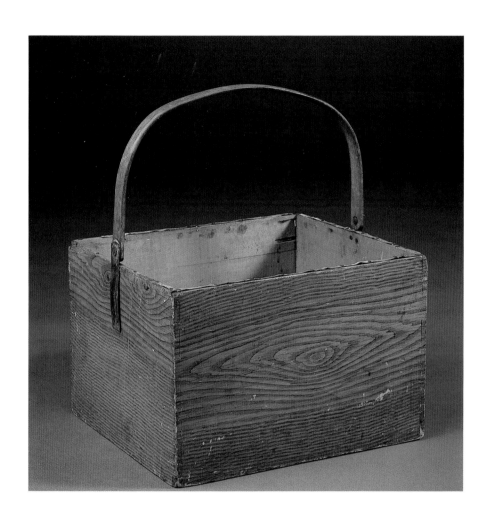

This kindling box is deceptively simple in its overall appearance and in the work involved in its construction. What looks like oak or another coarse-grained wood is actually lightweight basswood enlivened with a carefully applied painted finish to resemble wood grain. Never a common finish in Shaker communities, the use of decorative or contrasting woods is documented in journal accounts of the 1880s and 1890s. Certain extant objects, such as oval boxes, pegboards, interior doors and woodwork, and select pieces of furniture, display similar painted finish techniques. Some pegboard and one large cupboard in the Mount Lebanon Collection (see appendix, no. 5) are among other examples of this *faux* finish.

Rather than being nailed together, this lightweight box—its sides are only 5/16-inch thick—has its corners secured with dovetails. Its otherwise fragile top edge was once protected by a tin strip that was nailed in place. The gracefully curved and oval-shaped swing handle is secured at its pivot point with rivets attached to a brass strip, which in turn is fastened by smaller rivets to the sides of the box.

Forged iron
ca. 1820–1880
Tongs: 21 x 6 x 1 in.
Tongs: 19 1/2 x 2 3/4 x 1 in.
Dipper: 28 x 5 1/2 x 1 1/4 in.
Shovel: 21 1/2 x 4 1/2 x 1 1/8 in.
Poker: 27 x 2 1/4 x 3/4 in.

With both blacksmith and machine shops at Mount Lebanon, the Brothers were able to manufacture tools and machinery for other trades within the Shaker community: loom parts for weavers, press fixtures for printers, implements for those who worked the farms and orchards, hand tools for gardeners, and wagon and sleigh parts for wagoners. A significant portion of the blacksmiths' time was spent producing secondary parts for larger tools or objects, such as a pair of hinges or a latch for a cabinetmaker, or creating smaller tools, including tongs, shovels, and pokers for wood stoves. Probably the most visible of the blacksmiths' wares was the hardware that helped secure the Shakers' buildings. Hinges, handles, and latches were capably forged from hot iron. Blacksmiths employed their hammers, chisels, stakes, tongs, and anvils with a sensitivity that allowed simple objects to be transformed into subtle shapes and artistic forms.

63
Date stone

Marble
Carved: 1829.
1829
14 x 24 1/2 x 3 1/2 in.

64
Mortar

Marble
Carved on bottom: I,N,Y. 1828.
1828
4 x 8 x 18 in.

Most of the stonework at Mount Lebanon was related to the architecture of the Shaker village. Stone used in underground foundations was primarily found, field, or flat stone, but for portions of buildings aboveground stone was quarried nearby, cut or split to size, and brought by sled or wagon to the construction site. The 1829 date stone originated from the Brethren's shop of the North Family.

The mortar stone was used in conjunction with a now missing pestle, which was a round stone with a wood handle for pulverizing herbs. On the bottom is the date 1828 and the initials "I.N.Y.," those of Brother Isaac N. Youngs. Whether he made the mortar or was simply practicing lettering in stone is unknown. According to his own records, Brother Isaac did little stonework but was chosen to complete the lengthy lettering on two important pieces: the Fountain Stones that were erected at Mount Lebanon in 1842 and at Groveland, New York, the following year. Fountain Stones held important spiritual messages and were installed in the feast grounds where the Shakers held outdoor worship ceremonies during the revivalist period of the 1840s.

Specialized tools were often designed to help workers be more efficient or accurate while performing repetitious tasks. This angle-measuring device (left) has numerical divisions along its bottom edge, but it is not known what it was intended to measure. The scale here and on the quadrant could have been used to determine angles. Perhaps they were classroom aids or tools derived from the *Mechanic's Dictionary* and made for a specific Shaker trade. Their careful craftsmanship nevertheless displays the ingenuity of a Shaker "mechanic."

66
Woodworking tools

Jointer plane: Rock maple, steel
3 1/4 x 3 1/2 x 32 in. (body)
Backsaw: Beech, steel, brass
5 x 24 in.
Grooving plane: Beech, steel
2 1/4 x 3 x 14 in. (body)
Rabbet plane: Beech, steel
2 3/4 x 1 1/4 x 10 in. (body)
Rounding plane: Beech, steel
3 3/8 x 1 x 9 5/8 in. (not shown)
Brace: Beech, brass
4 3/4 x 13 3/4 x 1 in.

ca. 1820–1830

Even though Shaker furnituremakers incorporated much less decoration into their designs than did their counterparts in "the World," the tools they required were essentially the same. In fact, the Shakers purchased many of their tools commercially. Brother Freegift Wells of the neighboring community of Watervliet, New York, recorded several purchases of tools. One day in the early 1830s, he "spent 7 dollars 3 shillings & 9 p for tools, a plow, back saw, pocket rule, & plain irons." Years later, when setting up another workshop on May 26, 1857, he noted, "The Elder Br. Chauncy & myself sent to Albany & purchased part of a set of joiners tools for the elders shop." Believers also made many of their tools. On May 11, 1837, Brother Henry DeWitt recorded, "I helped David Rowley finish getting out his plain stock timber, 100 of them."

This group of basic tools contains pieces that were made by the Shakers or bear the marks of commercial manufacture. Whatever their origin, these tools were well crafted and carefully adjusted to assist the Brethren, such as Orren Haskins, David Rowley, Elisha Blakeman, and Amos Stewart, in creating the exceptional Shaker furniture we appreciate today.

Unidentified photographer, ca. 1900
Holding common woodworking tools, Charles Greaves (d. 1916) of the North Family is shown in work clothing typically worn by the Brothers.

67
Calipers

Ash, iron
ca. 1840
48 1/8 x 21 1/8 x 1 1/4 in.

Although tools such as these calipers were available commercially, this one was probably made by the Shakers. Such calipers were used when cutting timber or at the sawmill to measure the number of board feet of lumber in a plank or log.

From the early days of the Shakers' establishment, lumbering and sawmills were crucial to the temporal growth of the community. The availability of wood was crucial to many aspects of their livelihood, particularly the construction of buildings and furniture, and the development of industries, from coopering and the making of boxes and baskets to the production of chairs. Pine, yellow poplar, butternut, cherry, ash, and maple were all available locally at Mount Lebanon, although craftsmen even then complained of the decreasing quality and quantity of available materials.

The Shakers have been credited with the invention of the circular saw. Even if this is not so, as early as 1817 Shaker craftsmen recorded their use of circular saws and their refinement of planers and woodworking machines to facilitate their work. Five millponds were built at Mount Lebanon to provide adequate supplies of water for drinking, laundry, and the control of fires, as well as for powering several water wheels to run woodworking machinery.

68
Mangle roller

Maple
ca. 1840
40 3/8 x 3 1/2 in. diameter

With their progressive view toward the development of tools and machinery, and the immensity of the daily tasks that were involved in clothing and feeding scores of Believers, the Shakers refined many of the work processes that were handled by the Sisters. Among the many unique, hand-made tools in the Mount Lebanon Collection is this large maple roller, which was crafted for a specific purpose. It most likely was used to smooth cloth or linen in one of the laundry buildings. The finish-ing details of the handles, the scribe lines, and the crisp termina-tion of the handle to roller were carefully cut by the turner.

Photographs of the Shakers at work document other tools that were employed in the labor-inten-sive process of ironing the Shakers' clothing. In this photograph of the laundry building run by the North Family at Mount Lebanon, Brother Daniel Offord is seen in the background operating a press. A similar screw press is still found in the laundry building of the Shaker community at Sabbathday Lake, Maine.

69
Pitchfork

Oak
ca. 1830
55 x 12 3/4 in. (tine to tine)

Not unlike pitchforks made in "the World," this example was finely styled and crafted from a local material—oak. The craftsman likely shaped the tines while the wood was still green or applied heat and moisture to relax the wood enough to conform to its functional shape. One plane of the tines' graceful curve follows the arc of the farmer's swing as he lofted straw or hay into the barn. In another plane the craftsman bent the tines outward, broadening the pitchfork into a 12 3/4-inch-wide fork with three tines. Three dowels driven into holes drilled through the tines hold them apart to form this traditional farming tool.

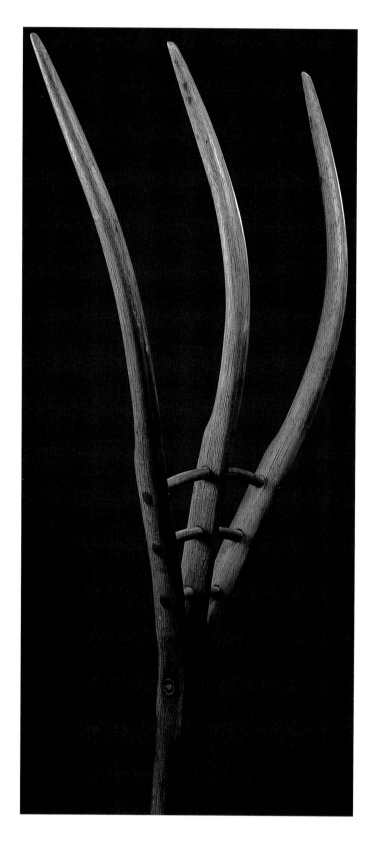

70, 71, 72
Grave markers

Cast iron
ca. 1870
51 1/2 x 17 3/8 x 2 in. (each)

With their aging membership and need for larger cemeteries, the Shakers were confronted with the dilemma of their inconsistent marking of graves. Prior to the installation of these unusual markers, plain slate or marble stones, sometimes carved with initials and a date, were used to mark graves. In response, these unique markers were devised, and similar ones still stand in the Shaker cemetery at Harvard, Massachusetts. As the Believers at Mount Lebanon recorded, "George Wickersham began putting up iron monuments in our cemetery as a remembrance of our departed Brethren and Sisters" (Western Reserve Historical Society, reel 32 220+).

The stakes were cast separately and fitted into a tapered dovetail on the back of the plate. Wood patterns were fabricated, with individual letters and numbers made for setting a person's name, age, and date of death. Most Shaker cemeteries, including that of the Church Family at Mount Lebanon, where these were obtained, now have a single, large memorial stone commemorating all the Brothers and Sisters of the United Society of Believers.

JEREMIH. TALCOTT
DIED. MAY. 1867.
AGED. 83.

POLLY. SMITH
DIED. OCT. 1867.
AGED. 69.

LUCY. DARROW
DIED. MARCH. 1870.
AGED. 91.

Lithograph, ink on paper, pine box
ca. 1870
5 x 22 x 9 1/2 in.

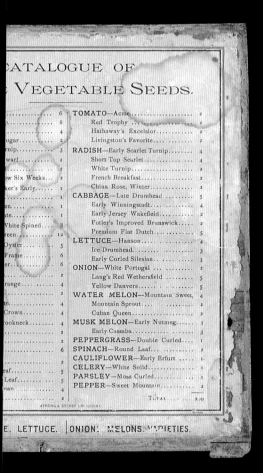

The Shakers are acknowledged as the first to use small paper envelopes or packets to hold and market garden seeds. According to extant account books, they systematically raised and marketed produce as early as 1795. Sales of seeds peaked in the 1860s and 1870s, and continued through the end of the century. Shakers in several northeastern communities—Sabbathday Lake, Maine; Enfield and Canterbury, New Hampshire; Watervliet, New York; Hancock, Massachusetts; and Mount Lebanon—raised and sold garden seeds. Their wholesale and retail sales were so extensive and aggressive that complaints had to be settled between competitive communities whose market areas overlapped. Numerous record books chronicle the variety and quantities of seeds sold by the Church Family at Mount Lebanon. Heavily illustrated gardening manuals were issued as early as 1835 for the retail trade.

Seed boxes were made by the hundreds. These simple, rectangular pine boxes with nailed or finger-jointed corners and bail wire hinges could be found in small country stores and large retail establishments throughout the region. Shaker peddlers traveled with wagonloads of Shaker-made products, including brooms and brushes, whips, baskets, oval boxes, and stacks of garden seed

numerous seed packets, but they also served as a colorful merchandising display.

The seed industry furnished seasonal employment for many Brothers and Sisters, from developing and planting seeds, to harvesting, counting, and sorting seeds, making and filling packages, and shipping the finished containers. On October 30, 1852, Brother Henry DeWitt noted his involvement in one small part of this elaborate process: "A new trade is now presented to my charge . . . which is to do the printing for the garden concerns and herb business, which will occupy nearly 9 month labor in a year" (Western Reserve Historical Society, Cleveland, VB 97).

74
Dried green sweet corn broadside

Letterpress process, ink, cardstock
ca. 1870
13 3/4 x 10 7/8 in.

Produced by the Crump Label Press in Chicago, this colorful broadside refers to one of Mount Lebanon's longest lasting industries, which operated from around 1830 until the end of the nineteenth century. An April 1879 issue of the journal *Shaker Manifesto* described the processing of dried green sweet corn. Huge quantities of sweet corn were contracted with local farmers. In the early years the corn was dried in the sun on platforms. By the late 1870s, however, much of the process was mechanized. After the corn was heated in a large steam cooker, three machines removed the corn from the cob. The kernels were then placed in shallow pans in two kilns and subjected to even heat for twenty-four hours. The dried corn was winnowed to remove the silk or husk. Lastly, it was packaged in small containers for the grocers' shelves or in barrels for the wholesale market. A large, round red label of similar design was probably applied to the end of the barrels. One exists in the collection of the Berkshire Atheneum in Pittsfield, Massachusetts.

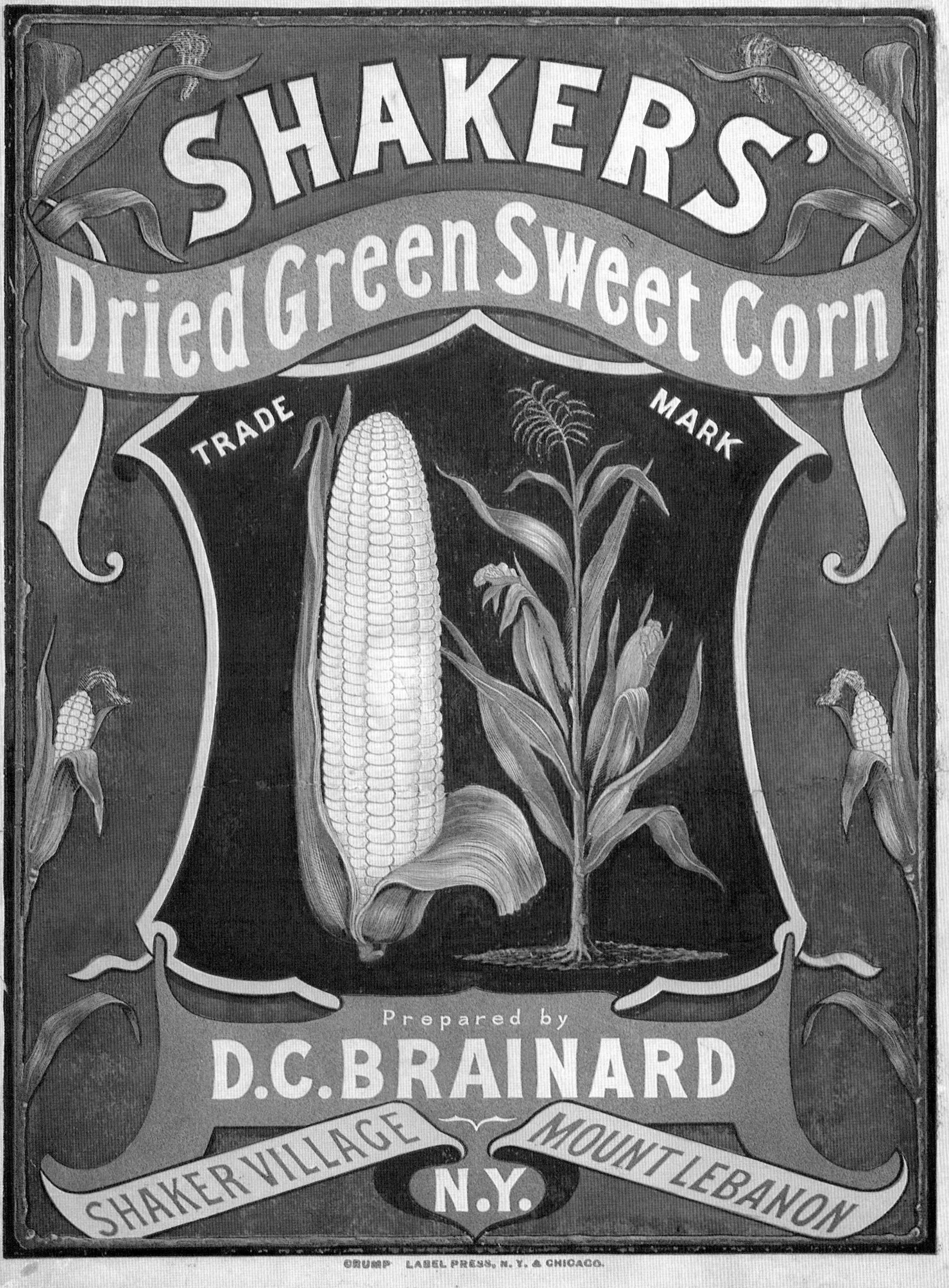

SHAKERS'
Dried Green Sweet Corn

TRADE   MARK

Prepared by
D.C. BRAINARD

SHAKER VILLAGE   MOUNT LEBANON
N.Y.

CRUMP LABEL PRESS, N.Y. & CHICAGO.

75
String beans label

Letterpress process, ink on paper
ca. 1890
4 1/2 x 14 in.

To identify and promote their products, the Shakers initially printed simple letterset paper labels (see cat. no. 77). These small labels gave only the product's name, using variations of lettering styles and different colors of ink. Later, as competitors employed larger and more colorful advertising materials, the Shakers selected bolder and more vibrant graphic designs that were printed on commercial lithographic presses. Some of their labels were possibly stock designs that were not specifically made for Shaker products. The label for fresh apples (cat. no. 76) differs only in text from a similar one that announces "FRESH APPLES / Andrew Croswell, Farmington Falls, Me." The printing firm evidently inserted a manufacturer's or processor's product and name into the already designed label. Another stock advertising label (private collection) dating from the early twentieth century features a Quaker girl to advertise Shaker processed apple products.

Probably one of the most intricate and colorful of these commercially lithographed labels that were used to sell Mount Lebanon products is this for string beans, which appears to combine original and stock design elements.

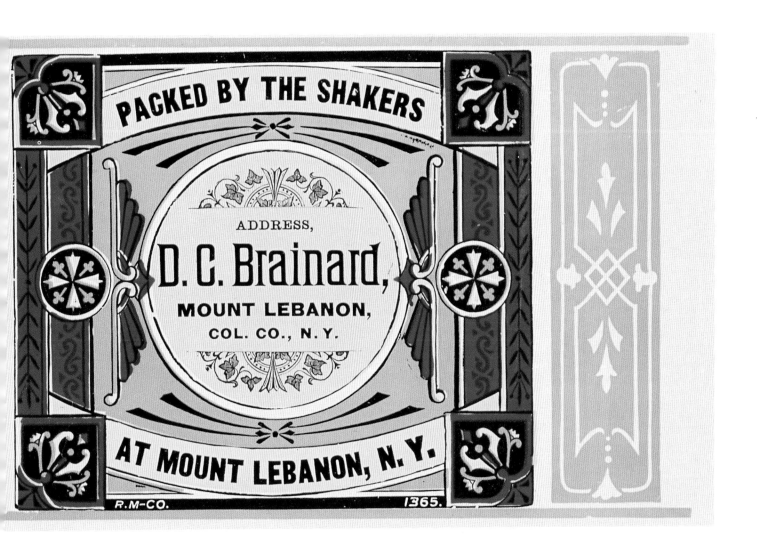

PACKED BY THE SHAKERS

ADDRESS,

D. C. Brainard,

MOUNT LEBANON,

COL. CO., N.Y.

AT MOUNT LEBANON, N.Y.

R.M-CO.   1365.

Brother Clinton Brainard (1828–1897) is best
known for his work in the Shaker food processing industries. His name is also displayed
on the labels of dried sweet corn and canned
apples.

76
Fresh apples label

Letterpress process, ink on paper
ca. 1890
6 1/4 x 19 1/4 in.

77
Applesauce label

Letterpress process, ink on paper
ca. 1850
5 x 10 in.

SHAKER FRUIT

PACKED AT

MOUNT LEBANON

COLUMBIA CO.,

N. Y.

SHAKERS'

APPLE SAUCE.

MANUFACTURED BY

Shakers, Mount Lebanon, N. Y.

Advertising and herb labels

Lithograph process, ink on paper
ca. 1870–1920

Seigel's Curative Syrup: 4 3/4 x 5 1/4 in.
Extract of Roots: 5 x 3 in.
Syrup of Bitter Bugle: 4 1/4 x 2 3/4 in.
Rose Water: 3 3/4 x 2 3/4 in.
Sundried Extract of Cicuta.: 2 1/4 x 3 3/4 in.
Extract of Sarsaparilla: 1 3/4 x 3 in.

The production of medicine occupied several Shaker communities, but the medicinal industry probably reached its highest level at Mount Lebanon. Medicinal products were grown and marketed there as early as the 1820s. By 1850 a building complex was constructed to provide space for the machinery, drying and storage facilities, and workrooms needed by the Brothers and Sisters. The herb processing building was discussed by editor William Procter in the January 1852 issue of the American *Journal of Pharmacy*. It was described as

a neat structure about 120 feet long by 38 feet wide, two stories high with a well lighted basement and airy garrett. . . . The basement is devoted to the pressing, grinding, and other heavy work, whilst at one end the steam boiler is placed. The first story is used for packing, papering, sorting, printing and storing the products, whilst the second story and loft are used exclusively for drying and storing. . . . The Society have three double presses in constant operation, and occasionally use two others. . . .
We were shown into the evaporating room where the vacuum apparatus is stationed. This consists of a globular copper vessel supported on cast iron columns attached to the floor.

The Shakers marketed some products through catalogue sales and sold others through wholesale and retail firms. A.J. White, proprietor of a pharmaceutical firm in New York City, developed a business relationship with the Shakers and extensively advertised their medicinal products. Seigel's Curative Syrup, Family Pills, and Smoothing Plasters were promoted in a series of sentimental trade cards. Almanacs included glowing testimonials of the effectiveness of Shaker medicines.

Photograph by William Winters, ca. 1931
The Shakers depended heavily on the income generated by the nationwide sale of their medicinal products, including extracts, pills, and plasters. Their most popular item was the Shaker extract of roots, later marketed as Mother Seigel's syrup. This complex of pharmaceutical buildings was operated by the Center Family.

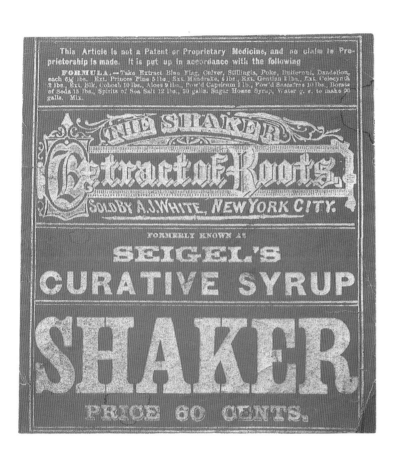

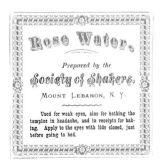

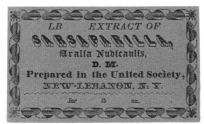

Labels needed for pressed herb wraps, bottles, tins, or card boxes were printed in both Shaker and commercial printshops. Some labels were bold and colorful, while others were simply informative. Large broadsides were created for prominent display by retailers. Contemporary advertising formats were frequently employed, as seen in these combinations of complex and decorative stock borders with an array of type styles and colored inks and papers.

Brown ink on blue-lined paper
ca. 1850s
12 x 10 in.
17 x 14 1/2 in. (with frame)

Accounts in the 1860s record from three to eight tons of solid and liquid extracts were prepared yearly. Account books and extant labels list hundreds of herbs and roots sold for their medicinal qualities: blackberry root, black alder bark, raspberry leaves, burdock root, dandelion, blood root comfrey, catnip, camomile, motherwort, horehound, scullcap, slippery elm, sage, wormwood, and sassafras bark.

80

Bottles with carrier

Pine, black paint, glass
ca. 1890
3 1/8 x 13 3/4 x 12 3/8 in.

Pottery, ceramic containers, and glass bottles in various sizes and shapes were purchased by the Shakers to market their products. Invoice and account books list numerous sources, including Dexter & Nellegar, Schieffelin Bros. & Co., and A.B. Sands & Co. The bottles were often embossed with the product's name, such as "Shaker Syrup," "Shaker Preparation," "Pearls of Ether," and "Shaker Family Pills." Paper labels provided instructions, dosage amounts, or information explaining what results to expect. As an illustration in the 1885 Almanac suggests (below), thousands of bottles must have been filled, sealed, and labeled daily, employing many Brothers and Sisters in the prosperous industry.

SHAKERESSES CORKING THE BOTTLES CONTAINING THE SHAKER EXTRACT
OF ROOTS, OR SEIGEL'S SYRUP.

5th MONTH.   **MAY, 1885.**

81
Height chart

Ink and pencil on paper
ca. 1860-1920
48 1/2 x 15 in.

This chart is certainly unique both as an artifact in itself and as a record of the specific heights of numerous Shaker Brothers and Sisters. The chart was found at Mount Lebanon fastened to a cupboard door, although this might not have been its original location. We can only speculate as to its importance or function, and it may have been a simple document kept for the Shakers' own curiosity and amusement. Included are the heights of scores of Shakers, among them Benjamin Gates, Emma Neale (at slightly under five feet), Hervey Eades (at under six feet), Elder Joseph Bracket (at 5'8"), and Henry Clough and Alonzo Hollister (both at 6'1"). Other heights range from 3'7" to 6'5". A few names are followed by dates, from 1862 to 1914, which indicate the chart was used over several decades. (See, for example, J. Winters 1869; Katie Wells, May 1891; and John Henry Calver, June 24, 1914.) The wide variety of signatures suggests each Shaker wrote his or her own name, which adds a further dimension of interest to this unusual historical record.

Ink on paper
ca. 1850
13 x 15 in.

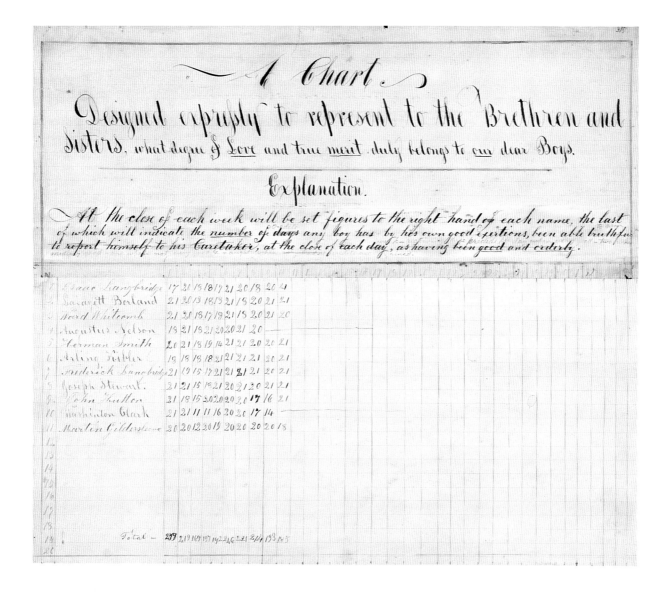

Family life within the Shaker community differed radically from that of the typical nuclear family. Hundreds of children were indentured to the United Society by their parents or guardians. Many children were orphans. Others were placed with the Shakers in the hope that their regulations and simple lifestyle would benefit the errant youth. All children, even those who entered the community when their natural parents joined the Shakers, were separated from adults and raised by several Brothers and Sisters. Around the age of fifteen they were moved to one of the many Families that composed the Shaker community.

Merit charts such as this may have been used to shape the character of children as part of their overall education. Practical training often took precedence, with girls learning sewing and cooking, and boys participating in carpentry, farm work, or one of the many trades operated by the Shakers.

This revised wording, pasted over the original text, and discovered during conservation, indicates the Shakers had to reconsider their policies toward monitoring behavior.

83
Motto

Watercolor and ink on paper
ca. 1880
9 1/2 x 12 1/2 in.
11 1/2 x 14 1/2 in. (with frame)

Inspirational sayings have long been part of the rememberances that people have collected. The source of this Shaker motto is unknown, although its meaning reflects the humanitarian spirit that prevailed at Mount Lebanon in the years from 1850 to 1880 under the guidance of Brother Frederick Evans and Sisters Anna White and Antoinette Doolittle. *Testimonies of the Life, Character, Revelations and Doctrines of Our Ever Blessed Mother Ann Lee, and the Elders with her,* first published in 1816, contains many sayings that were collected by Believers who personally knew Mother Ann and wanted to share her inspiration with others. During the Victorian era, calendars, maps, and sayings hung on the walls of many Shaker rooms. Historic photographs indicate that early rules deploring the decoration of interior walls were being relaxed, and an inspirational saying such as this became a common sight in Shaker dwellings and buildings.

84
Hymn book

Leather, paper, ink
ca. 1840
5 1/2 x 5 1/4 in.

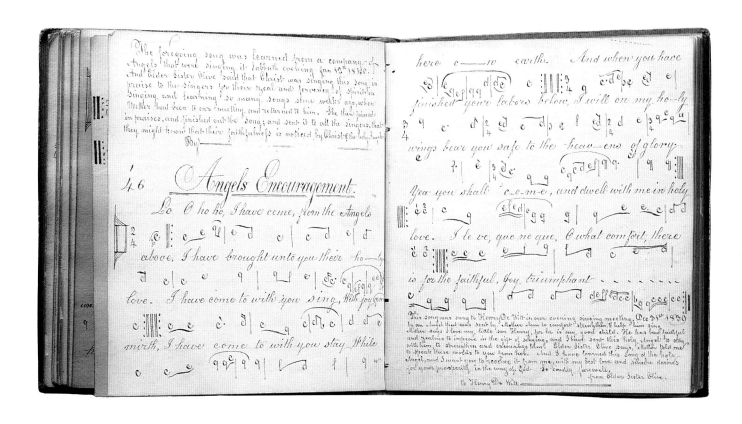

Characteristic of much written Shaker music is the use of an unusual notation system of letters to record and duplicate their vast quantity of "gift songs." In the late 1830s and early 1840s, thousands of gift songs were received through "instruments," persons who were given messages from the spirit world. Many of these songs were transcribed by hand into hymn books, such as this one. In 1843 Isaac N. Youngs assisted his Brothers and Sisters in reading music by publishing a manual that employed a system of letters in place of musical notes.

In addition to music, other gifts were received in the form of spirit drawings. These fanciful, colorful drawings intertwined geometric forms with depictions of birds, fruit, and leaves. Their texts described the inspired visions that had been received during the era of spiritual revivalism.

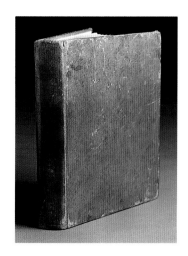

85

Desk set and glasses

Leather, blue-lined paper, glass,
metal, linen
ca. 1930
Blotter: 9 1/4 x 18 3/4 in.
Glasses: 1 x 4 1/2 in.
Glasses case: 6 1/2 x 1 in.
Handkerchief: 7 x 8 in.
Case: 8 x 2 1/2 in.

Judging by the initials on this desk
set and glasses case, these items
belonged to Sadie and Emma
Neale. These natural sisters were
brought to Mount Lebanon at the
ages of six and eight, and they
spent their entire lives as Shaker
Sisters there and in the communities at Watervliet and Hancock.

In their book *Fruits of the Shaker
Tree of Life,* collectors Edward and
Faith Andrews spoke affectionately of Sister Sadie, who they
knew through their extensive
dealings with the elderly Shakers.
In her last letter written to them
on April 5, 1945, Sister Sadie
spoke of the nearing end of her
long life, and in a sense of the
closing of the community at
Mount Lebanon.

Dear Friends:

*Yours was duly received, and was not
I pleased. We had a very pleasant
Easter, but a very quiet one. No one
came to see and we went to see no
one—but we were happy among ourselves. . . . We may have some set-
backs but we can put up with these.
We cannot expect to have anything
settled, even the weather, while the
country is in its present condition.
Some are talking Peace, but I do not
see it yet. . . . Roberts is still making
[oval] boxes for me when he can get
material to work with . . . but I am
nearing the end of my journey and
shall not miss these things much
longer. . . . I hope to see you once
more. Now as I have nothing more
[worth] writing about, I will love you
and leave you in peace . . . ever yours.*

Affectionately

Sadie

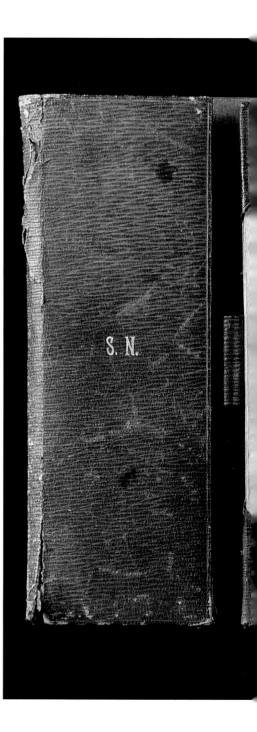

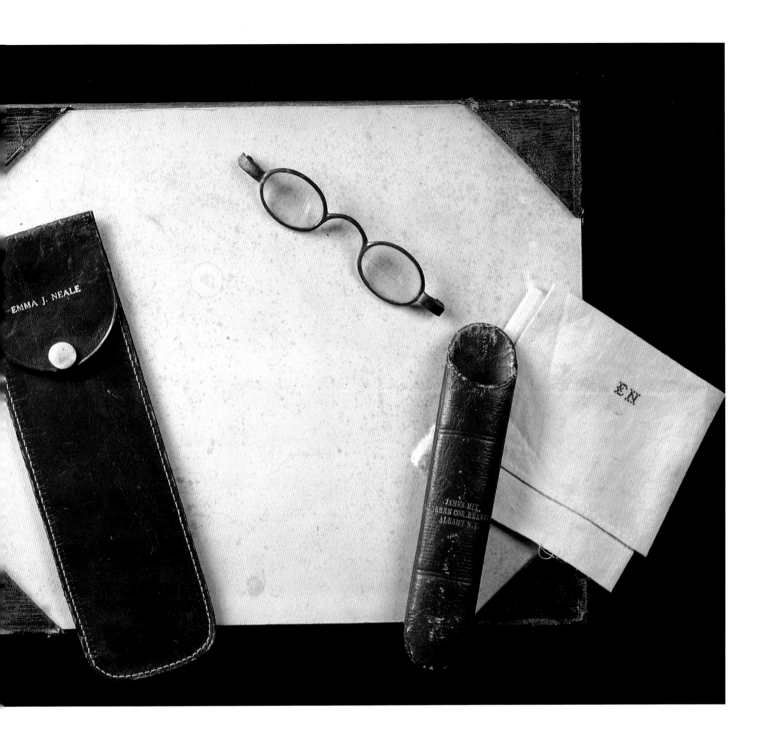

Joining the community of Believers at the ages of eight and six, respectively, Emma and Sadie Neale lived the rest of their long lives as Shakers. As both natural and Shaker sisters, Emma and Sadie were often photographed together.

Unidentified photography studio, ca. 1900
Sister Sadie (Sarah) Neale (1849–1948)

Photograph by Simmons, Pittsfield, Massachusetts, ca. 1890
Sister Emma Neale (1847–1943)

86
Ann Lee cottage sign

Ink on paper
ca. 1920?
11 x 14 in.

Previously a Shaker dwelling dating from 1835, the Ann Lee cottage was opened by Sister Emma Neale in 1906 as a way to provide accommodations to boarders and to bring income into the community at Mount Lebanon. Closing the cottage, as announced in this undated broadside, foretold many changes that eventually led to the decline and inevitable closing of Mount Lebanon.

Although most of the property had been sold several years earlier to the New Lebanon School for Boys (later renamed the Darrow School), Mount Lebanon as a Shaker community closed more officially on October 15, 1947, when the last of the remaining Shakers were relocated to Hancock, across the state line. This marked the end of Mount Lebanon's role as the principal seat of authority of the United Society of Believers, a position it had held for more than 160 years.

THE ANN LEE COTTAGE

Mount Lebanon, N. Y.

Will NOT Be Open To Boarders This Season.

E. J. NEALE.

APPENDIX

A selection of other
pieces in the
Mount Lebanon
Shaker Collection

1
Cupboard over drawers
Pine, walnut, hardwood
knobs, brass hinges
ca. 1860
77 1/2 x 74 1/2 x 23 in.

2
Counter
Pine, poplar, hardwood
knobs
ca. 1830
33 1/8 x 71 x 31 1/2 in.

3
Cupboard over drawers
Pine, hardwood knobs
ca. 1840
76 1/4 x 54 1/2 x 24 in.

4
Counter
Pine, hardwood knobs
ca. 1830
68 x 30 1/2 x 34 in.

5
Cupboard with
sliding doors
Pine, hardwood knobs
ca. 1870
81 1/2 x 69 x 24 in.

6
Case of drawers
Pine, cherry
ca. 1830
39 1/2 x 127 1/2 x
30 1/2 in.

7
Case of drawers
Built by Orren Haskins
Pine, butternut,
hardwood knobs
1847
33 x 104 x 32 in.
Signed: OH / March
1847

8
Cupboard over
drawers
Pine, poplar,
hardwood knobs
ca. 1840
94 x 85 x 18 1/2 in.

9
Library cupboard
Built by George
Wickersham
Poplar, walnut, porcelain
knobs, brass, glass
ca. 1880
91 x 113 1/2 x 13 1/2 in.

12
Desk
Pine, hardwood knobs
ca. 1860
29 1/2 x 87 x 23 1/2 in.

10
Work bench
Built by Orren Haskins
Pine, butternut, birch
1853
30 1/2 x 189 x 39 in.
Signed: OH / 1853

13
Kitchen
Marble, iron
ca. 1827
Now installed at Hancock
Shaker Village

11
Cupboard
Pine, hardwood knobs
ca. 1820
90 1/2 x 72 1/2 x 25 1/2 in.

SELECT BIBLIOGRAPHY

SHAKER SOURCES

Bishop, Rufus, and Seth Youngs Wells, eds. *Testimonies of the Life, Character, Revelations and Doctrines of our Ever Blessed Mother Ann Lee. . . .* Hancock, Massachusetts: J. Tallcott & J. Deming, June 15, 1816. 2d ed., revised by Giles B. Avery. Albany: Weed, Parsons, 1888.

Blinn, Henry C. "A Journey to Kentucky in the Year 1873." Reprinted in *The Shaker Quarterly* 5–7, no. 1 (Spring 1965–Spring 1967).

Elkins, Hervey. *Fifteen Years in the Senior Order of Shakers.* Hanover, New Hampshire: Dartmouth Press, 1953.

Green, Calvin, and Seth Youngs Wells. *A Summary View of the Millennial Church or United Society of Believers. . . .* Albany: Packard & Van Benthuysen, 1823.

Johnson, Brother Theodore E. *Hands to Work and Hearts to God.* Brunswick, Maine: Bowdoin College of Art, 1969.

List of Believers at the Various Shaker Communities. Western Reserve Historical Society, Shaker Collection, Cleveland, Ohio. Microfilm, reel 123.

The Manifesto 1–29, January 1871–December 1899. [East Canterbury, New Hampshire: United Societies, 1871–1899.] Published monthly, in 1871–1872 by the Mount Lebanon Bishopric as *The Shaker;* in 1873–1875 by the United Society as *Shaker and Shakeress;* in 1876–1877 by the Canterbury Shakers, Henry Clay Blinn, editor, as *The Shaker;* in 1878–1882 as *The Shaker Manifesto;* in 1883–1899 as *The Manifesto.* Archives, Canterbury Shaker Village, Canterbury, New Hampshire.

[Meacham, Joseph.] "Collection of Writings Concerning Church Order and Government," 1791–1796 [copied by Rufus Bishop, 1850]. Western Reserve Historical Society, Shaker Collection, Cleveland, Ohio.

"Millennial Laws of Gospel Statutes and Ordinances Adopted to the Day of Christ's Second Appearing." Revised and re-established by the Ministry and Elders, October 1845. Reprinted in Andrews, *The People Called Shakers,* pp. 253–289.

"'Millennial Laws' of 1821." Edited and with an introduction by Theodore E. Johnson, *Shaker Quarterly* 7, no. 2 (Summer 1967), pp. 35–58.

[Wells, Seth Youngs.] *Testimonies Concerning the Character and Ministry of Mother Ann Lee and the First Witness of the Gospel of Christ's Second Appearing. . . .* Albany: Packard & Van Benthuysen, 1827. Andrews Shaker Collection, Henry Frances du Pont Winterthur Museum, Winterthur, Delaware.

White, Anna, and Leila S. Taylor. *Shakerism, Its Meaning and Message.* Columbus, Ohio: Fred J. Herr, 1904.

Youngs, Isaac N. "A Domestic Journal of Daily Occurrences," Church Family, Mount Lebanon, New York. New York State Library, Shaker Collection, Albany, 13500.

BOOKS AND ARTICLES

Andrews, Edward Deming. *The Community Industries of the Shakers.* New York State Museum Handbook, no. 15. Albany: University of the State of New York, 1933.

_____. *The People Called Shakers.* New York: Oxford University Press, 1953.

Andrews, Edward Deming, and Faith Andrews. *Religion in Wood: A Book of Shaker Furniture.* Bloomington: Indiana University Press, 1937.

_____. *Shaker Furniture: The Craftsmanship of an American Communal Sect.* New Haven: Yale University Press, 1937.

_____. *Work and Worship: The Economic Order of the Shakers.* Greenwich, Connecticut: New York Graphic Society, 1974.

_____. *Fruits of the Shaker Tree of Life.* Stockbridge, Massachusetts: Berkshire Traveller Press, 1975.

Brewer, Priscilla J. *Shaker Communities, Shaker Lives.* Hanover, New Hampshire: University Press of New England, 1986.

Burns, Amy Stechler, and Ken Burns. *The Shakers: Hands to Work Hearts to God.* New York: Portland House, 1987.

Emlen, Robert P. *Shaker Village Views: Illustrated Maps and Landscape Drawings by Shaker Artists of the Nineteenth Century.* Hanover, New Hampshire: University Press of New England, 1987.

Emerich, A.D., and Arlen Benning. *Shaker: Furniture and Objects from the Faith and Edward Deming Andrews Collections.* Washington, D.C.: Smithsonian Institution Press, published for The Renwick Gallery of the National Collections of Fine Arts, 1973.

Flint, Charles L. *Mount Lebanon Shaker Collection.* New Lebanon, New York: Mount Lebanon Shaker Village, 1987.

Gibbs, James W., and Robert W. Meader. *Shaker Clock Makers.* Columbia, Pennsylvania: The National Association of Watch and Clock Collectors.

Gifford, Don, ed. *An Early View of the Shakers: Benson John Lossing and the "Harper's" Article of July 1857.* Hanover, New Hampshire: University Press of New England, 1989.

Gordon, Beverly. *Shaker Textile Arts.* Hanover, New Hampshire: University Press of New England, 1980.

Grant, Jerry V., and Douglas R. Allen. *Shaker Furniture Makers.* Hanover, New Hampshire: University Press of New England. Published for Hancock Shaker Village, Inc., Pittsfield, Massachusetts, 1989.

Kassay, John. *The Book of Shaker Furniture.* Amherst: University of Massachusetts, 1980.

McKinstry, E. Richard, comp. *The Edward Deming Andrews Memorial Shaker Collection.* New York: Garland, 1987.

Meader, Robert F.W. *Illustrated Guide to Shaker Furniture.* New York: Dover, 1982.

Miller, M. Stephen. *A Century of Shaker Ephemera.* New Britain, Connecticut: M. Stephen Miller, 1988.

Morse, Flo. *The Shakers and the World's People.* Hanover, New Hampshire: University Press of New England, 1987.

Muller, Charles R. *The Shaker Way.* Worthington: Ohio Antique Review, 1979.

Muller, Charles R., and Timothy D. Rieman. *The Shaker Chair.* Winchester, Ohio: Canal Press, 1984.

Nordhoff, Charles. *The Communistic Societies of the United States. . . .* New York: Harper & Brothers, 1875.

Richmond, Mary L. *Shaker Literature, A Bibliography.* Vols. 1 and 2. Hancock, Massachusetts: Shaker Community, Inc., 1977.

Rieman, Timothy D., and Jean M. Burks. *The Complete Book of Shaker Furniture.* New York: Harry N. Abrams, Inc., 1993.

Scherer, John L. *New York Furniture at the New York State Museum.* Alexandria, Virginia: Highland House, 1984.

Shea, John G. *The American Shakers and Their Furniture, with Measured Drawings of Museum Classics.* New York: Van Nostrand Reinhold, 1971.

Sprigg, June. *By Shaker Hands.* New York: Alfred A. Knopf, 1975.

_____. *Inner Light: The Shaker Legacy.* New York: Alfred A. Knopf, 1985

_____. *Shaker: Masterworks of Utilitarian Design Created between 1800 and 1875 by the Master Craftsmen and Craftswomen of America's Foremost Communal Religious Sect.* Exhibition catalogue. Katonah, New York: Katonah Gallery, 1983.

_____. *Shaker Design.* Exhibition catalogue. New York: Whitney Museum of American Art, 1986.

_____. *Shaker: Original Paints and Patinas.* Allentown, Pennsylvania: Muhlenberg College for the Arts, 1987.

Sprigg, June, and Jim Johnson. *Shaker Woodenware: A Field Guide.* Vol.1 Berkshire House: Great Barrington, Massachusetts, 1991.

Sprigg, June, and David Larkin. *Shaker: Life, Work, and Art.* New York: Stewart, Tabori and Chang, 1987.

Stein, Stephen J. *The Shaker Experience in America.* New Haven: Yale University Press, 1992.

Wertkin, Gerard C. *The Four Seasons of Shaker Life.* New York: Simon and Schuster, 1986.